Weather Lore

Volume III

The Elements

M
S
P

Richard Inwards

Weather Lore

A Collection of

Proverbs, Sayings & Rules

Concerning the Weather

Volume III

The Elements -

Clouds, Mists, Haze, Dew, Fog, Rain, Rainbows

PAPADAKIS

Published in Great Britain in 2013 by
Papadakis Publisher

PAPADAKIS

An imprint of New Architecture Group Limited

Kimber Studio, Winterbourne, Berkshire, RG20 8AN, UK
info@papadakis.net | www.papadakis.net

@papadakisbooks PapadakisPublisher

Publishing Director: Alexandra Papadakis
Design: Alexandra Papadakis
Editorial Assistant: Juliana Kassianos

First published in 1898 by Elliot Stock, 62 Paternoster Row, London

ISBN 978 1 906506 39 1

We gratefully acknowledge the permission granted to use these images. Every possible attempt has been made to identify and contact copyright holders. Any errors or omissions are inadvertent and will be corrected in subsequent editions.

A CIP catalogue of this book is available from the British Library

Printed and bound in China

Contents

A
A'
B
B'

Clouds - An Introduction

As it will be seen, much is to be gleaned by observing the forms and appearances of clouds. By Howard, Fitzroy, and others these masses of vapour have been marshalled in the order of their formation and altitude, so that the most casual observer may soon judge of the age of a cloud, whether seen as a light, filmy cirrus, or in the form of a dark, threatening nimbus, ripe for rain, and spreading like a vampire's wing over the landscape.

Although the names given by Howard to the different clouds have been here adopted, and the same general arrangement maintained, yet the familiar names given to these masses of vapour by sailors and others, such as Mackerel Sky, Mares' Tails, Wool Bags, etc., have not been omitted. Clouds should of course be observed with a proper allowance for the force and direction of the wind at the time. With a swift upper current of air a clear sky sometimes becomes obscured in a few minutes, whilst in calmer weather changes in the appearance of the sky are slow to occur, and can be reckoned on with more safety.

Clouds

And now the mists from earth are clouds in heaven,
Clouds slowly castellating in a calm
Sublimer than a storm, while brighter breathes
O'er the whole firmament the breadth of blue,
Because of that excessive purity
Of all those hanging snow-white palaces:
A gentle contrast, but with power divine.
- Wilson.

While any of the clouds, except the nimbus, retain their primitive forms, no rain can take place; and it is by observing the changes and transitions of cloud form that weather may be predicted.
- Howard.

Form

The higher the clouds, the finer the weather.

High

When on clear days isolated clouds drive over the zenith from the rain-wind side, storm and rain follow within twenty-four hours.
- United States.

Isolated

After clouds calm weather.
- T. Fuller.

Calm

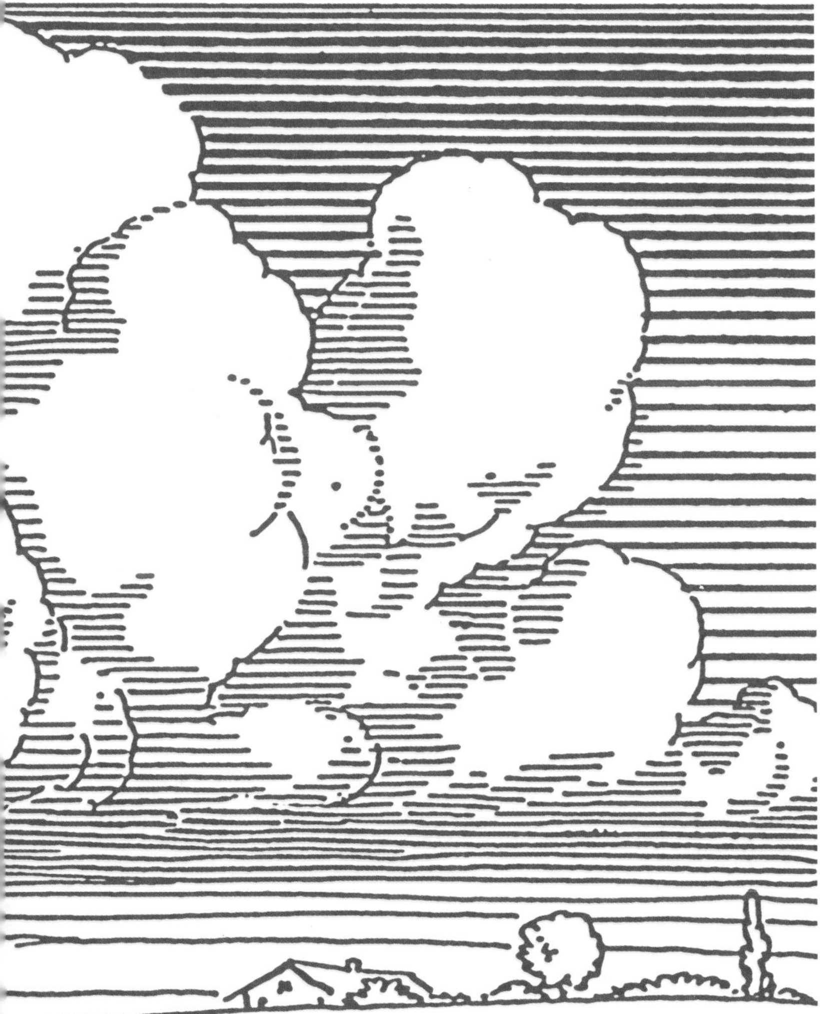

Dark — Clouds that the sun builds up darken him.

With wind — It will not rain much so long as the sky is clear before the wind; but when clouds fall in against the wind, rain will soon follow.

When clouds break before the wind, leaving a clear sky, fine weather will follow.

Indications of — After fine, clear weather the first signs in the sky of a coming change are usually light streaks, curls, wisps, or mottled patches of white distant clouds, which increase and are followed by an overcasting of murky vapour that grows into cloudiness. The appearance more or less oily or watery, as wind or rain may prevail, is an infallible sign. Usually the higher and more distant such clouds seem to be, the more gradual, but general, the coming change of weather will prove.
- Fitzroy.

Growth of — Now clouds combine, and spread o'er all the sky,
When little rugged parts ascend on high,
Which may be twined, though by a feeble tie;
These make small clouds, which, driven on by wind,
To other like and little clouds are joined,
And these increase by more: at last they form
Thick, heavy clouds; and thence proceeds a storm.
- Lucretius (Creech).

Dispersing — When clouds, after rain, disperse during the night, weather will not remain clear.

Can any understand the spreadings of the clouds? - Job xxxvi. 29. Spreading

Dost thou know the balancing of the clouds? - Job xxxvii. 16. Balancing

Bleak is the morn when blows the north from high; Dawn
Oft when the dawnlight paints the starry sky,
A misty cloud suspended hovers o'er
Heaven's blessed earth with fertilizing store,
Drained from the living streams: aloft in air
The whirling winds the buoyant vapour bear,
Resolved at eve in rain or gusty cold,
As by the north the troubled rack is rolled.
- Hesiod (Elton).

Clouds without rain in summer indicate wind. Without rain
- Theophrastus ("Signs, etc." J. G. Wood's Translation).

Cloudy mornings turn to clear evenings. Morning

When the clouds of the morn to the west fly away,
You may conclude on a settled, fair day.

At sunset with a cloud so black, Evening
A westerly wind you shall not lack.

Many small clouds at north-west in the evening show that rain is gathering, and will suddenly fall.
- Pointer.

Storm cloud — When a heavy cloud comes up in the south-west, and seems to settle back again, look out for a storm.

Accumulating — If the sky, from being clear, becomes fretted or spotted all over with bunches of clouds, rain will soon fall.
- Shepherd of Banbury.

Stationary — When clouds are stationary and others accumulate by them, but the first remain still, it is a sign of a storm.
- Theophrastus ("Signs, etc." J. G. Wood's Translation).

Low — If on the ocean's bosom clouds appear,
While the blue vault above is bright and clear,
These signs by shepherds and by sailors seen,
Give pleasing hope of days and nights serene.
- Aratus (J. Lamb).

Increasing — If clouds increase visibly, and the clear sky become less, it is a sign of rain.

Like inconstant clouds
That, rack'd upon the carriage of the winds,
Increase.
- Play of King Edward III.
(Sometimes attributed to Shakespeare.)

If the clouds appear to drive fast when there is no wind, expect wind from that quarter from which they are driven. But if they gather and collect together, on the sun's approach to that part, they will begin to disperse; and then if they disperse towards the north, it prognosticates wind; if towards the south, rain.
- Bacon.

Collecting and driving

When the carry [current of clouds] gaes west,
Gude weather is past;
When the carry gaes east,
Gude weather comes neist.

Driving

When ye see a cloud rise out of the west, straightway ye say, There cometh a shower; and so it is. - Luke xii. 54.

From west

Fear not as much a cloud from the land as from ocean in winter; but in the summer a cloud from a darkling coast is a warning.
- Theophrastus ("On Winds" J. G. Wood's Translation).

If the sky clears, and the clouds commence to break in the quarter opposite the wind, it will be fine; but if it clear up to windward, it indicates nothing, and leaves the weather uncertain. - Bacon.

Clearing

With mock suns

If clouds shall have shut in the sun, the less light there is left, and the smaller the sun's orb appears, the more severe will the storm prove. But if the disc of the sun appear double or treble, as if there were two or three suns, the storm will be much more violent, and will last many days.
- Bacon.

North-west

If the upper current of clouds comes from the north-west in the morning, a fine day will ensue.

If in the north-west before daylight end there appear a company of small black clouds like flocks of sheep, it is a sure and certain sign of rain.
- Wing, 1649.

If a layer of thin clouds drive up from the north-west, and under other clouds moving more to the south, expect fine weather.
- United States.

In winter and in the North Atlantic a cloud rising from the north-west is an infallible forerunner of a great tempest.
- Kalm ("Travels").

East

Clouds in the east,
obscuring the sun,
indicate fair weather.

In the North Atlantic, if clouds appear during an easterly wind to the south-west, with their points turning to the north-east, it is a sign of a south-west wind in twenty-four hours.
- Kalm (Travels).

South

If clouds drive up high from the south, expect a thaw.

South-west

Small scattering clouds flying high in the south-west foreshow whirlwinds.
- Howard.

High

A sky covered with clouds need not cause apprehension, if the latter are high, and of no great density, and the air is still, the barometer at the same time being high. Rain falling under such circumstances is generally light, or of not long continuance. - Jenyns.

Dark

If high, dark clouds are seen in spring, winter, or fall, expect cold weather.

Dark heavy clouds, carried rapidly along near the earth, are a sign of great disturbance in the atmosphere from conflicting currents. At such times the weather is never settled, and rain extremely probable.
- Jenyns.

Diverging

If the clouds, as they come forward, seem to diverge from a point in the horizon, a wind may be expected from that quarter, or the opposite.
- Thomas Best.

Apparently stationary

The apparent permanency and stationary aspect of a cloud is often an optical deception, arising from the solution of vapour on one side of a given point, while it is precipitated on the other.
- J. F. Daniels.

Against heavy rain every cloud rises bigger than the preceding, and all are in a growing state.
- G. Adams.

Rising

Clouds floating low, and casting shadows on the ground, are usually followed by rain.
- United States.

Low

High upper clouds, crossing the sun, moon, or stars in direction different from that of the lower clouds, or the wind then felt below, foretell a change of wind toward their direction.
- Fitzroy.

Motions of

When the generality of the clouds rack or drive with the wind (though there are many in little fleeces, or long strakes lying higher, and appearing not to move), the wind is flagging, and will quickly change and shift its point. - Pointer.

In layers

If two strata of clouds appear in hot weather to move in different directions, they indicate thunder.

If, during dry weather, two layers of clouds appear moving in opposite directions, rain will follow.

Clouds floating at different heights show different currents of air, and the upper one generally prevails. If this is north-east, fine weather may be expected; if south-west, rain.
- C. L. Prince.

Cross wind

If you see clouds going across the wind, there is a storm in the air.

If clouds float at different heights and rates, but generally in opposite directions, expect heavy rains.

Gusts

If there be a cloudy sky, with dark clouds driving fast under higher clouds, expect violent gusts of wind.

Red

Red clouds at sunrise foretell wind; at sunset, a fine day for the morrow. - Bacon.

Narrow, horizontal, red clouds after sunset in the west indicate rain before thirty-six hours.
Red clouds in the east, rain the next day.

Greenish

When you observe greenish tinted masses of composite cloud collect in the south-east and remain there for several hours, expect a succession of heavy rains and gales. - C. L. Prince.

After black clouds, clear weather. Black

Dark clouds in the west at sunrise indicate rain on that day.

Clay-coloured and muddy clouds portend rain and wind. Dull
- Bacon.

Clouds before sunset of an amber or a gold colour, and with gilt fringes, after the sun has sunk lower, foretell fine weather. Golden
- Bacon.

The wind-gale or prismatic colouring of the clouds is considered by sailors a sign of rain. Colouring

Light, delicate, quiet tints or colours, with soft, undefined forms of clouds, indicate and accompany fine weather; but unusual or gaudy hues, with hard, definitely outlined clouds, foretell rain, and probably strong wind. - Fitzroy.

Brassy — Brassy-coloured clouds in the west at sunset indicate wind.

Dusky — Dusky or tarnished silver-coloured clouds indicate hail. - Howard.

Scud — Small, inky-looking clouds foretell rain; light scud clouds driving across heavy masses show wind and rain, but if alone may indicate wind only.
- Fitzroy.

Bright and dark — If clouds be bright,
'Twill clear to-night;
If clouds be dark,
'Twill rain - do you hark?

White — If the cloud be like in colour to a white skin, it is a sign of a storm.
- Theophrastus ("Signs, etc." J. G. Wood's Translation).

Clouds above - water below.

Rain

He causeth the vapours to ascend from the ends of
the earth;
He maketh lightnings for the rain;
He bringeth the wind out of His treasuries.
- Psalm cxxxv. 7.

Storm

Generally squalls are preceded, or accompanied, or followed by clouds; but the dangerous white squall of the West Indies is indicated only by a rushing sound and by white wave crests to windward.
- Fitzroy.

A squall cloud that one sees through or under is not likely to bring or be accompanied by so much wind as a dark, continued cloud extending beyond the horizon.
- Fitzroy.

Against wind

If you see a cloud rise against the wind or side-wind, when that cloud comes up to you, the wind will blow the same way that the cloud came; and the same rule holds good of a clear place when all the sky is equally thick, except one clear edge.
- Shepherd of Banbury.

Increasing

A small increasing white cloud about the size of a hand to windward is a sure precursor of a storm.

A small, fast-growing black cloud in violent motion, seen in the tropics, is called the "bull's eye", and precedes the most terrible hurricanes.

Description of

Sometimes we see a cloud that's dragonish,
A vapour sometimes like a bear or lion,
A towered citadel, a pendent rock,
A forked mountain, a blue promontory
With trees upon't that nod unto the world
And mock our eyes with air.
That which is now a horse, even with a thought
The rack dislimns and makes it indistinct
As water is in water.
- Shakespeare (Antony and Cleopatra).

Increasing

Behold, there ariseth a little cloud out of the sea, like a man's hand... Prepare thy chariot, and get thee down, that the rain stop thee not. And it came to pass that the heaven was black with clouds and wind, and there was a great rain.
- 1 Kings xviii. 44, 45.

Bank

A bench (or bank) of clouds in the west means rain.
- Surrey.

Broken

When small dark clouds (broken nimbi) appear against a patch of blue sky, there will be rain before sunset.
- C. L. Prince.

CIRRUS
Definition

Parallel, flexuous, or diverging fibres, extensible in any or all directions.
- Howard.

Common names:
Curl Cloud,
Mares' Tails,
Goat's Hair, etc.
- T. Forster.

Indicating change

After a long run of clear weather the appearance of light streaks of cirrus cloud at a great elevation is often the first sign of change.
- Jenyns.

Indicating wind

Long parallel bands of clouds in the direction of the wind indicate steady high winds to come.

Feathery clouds, like palm branches or the "fleur de lis", denote immediate or coming showers.
- Bacon.

Showery

If cirrus clouds dissolve and appear to vanish, it is an indication of fine weather.

Fine weather

Rain — If the cirrus clouds appear to windward, and change to cirro-stratus, it is a sign of rain.

Sheet cirrus — Sheet cirrus occurs with southerly and westerly, but rarely with steady northerly or north-easterly, winds, unless a change to a westerly or southerly quarter is approaching. - Hon. F. A. R. Russell.

Rain — In unsettled weather sheet cirrus precedes more wind or rain.

The longer the dry weather has lasted, the less is rain likely to follow the cloudiness of cirrus.

Murky — A large formation of murky white cirrus may merely indicate a backing of wind to an easterly quarter.

Feathery — If a shower be approaching from the west, it may be seen shooting forth white feathery rays from its upper edge, often very irregular and crooked.

Cirrus of a long, straight, feathery kind, with soft edges and outlines, or with soft, delicate colours at sunrise and sunset, is a sign of fine weather.

Curdled cirrus

This cloud often indicates the approach of bad weather.

Bar or ribbed cirrus

The rapid movement of a cloud, something between cirrus and cirro-cumulus, in distinct dense bars, in a direction at right angles to the length of the bars, is, by itself, a certain sign of a gale of wind. If the bars are sharply defined and close together, the severer will be the storm. Sometimes these bars remind one of the form of a gridiron. The bands move transversely, and generally precede the storm by from twelve to forty-eight hours.
- Hon. F. A. R. Russell.

Curled

Curly wisps and blown-back pieces are not a bad sign.

Tails downwards	When the tails are turned downwards, fair weather or slight showers often follow.
Definite	The harder and more distinct the outline, and the more frequently particular forms are repeated, the worse the result.
Fibrous	Long, hard, greasy-looking streaks, with rounded edges or knobs, whether crossed by fibres at right angles or not, are a sign of storms; but the storms may be at a distance.
	Cottony shreds, rounded and clear in outline, indicate dangerous disturbances.
Tufty	Regular, wavy tufts, with or without cross lines, are bad, especially if the tufts end, not in fibres, but in rounded knobs.
Regular	Feathery cirrus in thick patches at equal distances apart is a sign of storm; so is any appearance of definite waves of alternate sky and cloud; so is any regular repetition of the same form.
Undulating	Slightly undulating lines of cirrus occur in fine weather; but anything like a deeply indented outline precedes heavy rain or wind.
Twisted	Cirrus simply twisted or in zigzag lines of a fibrous character often appears in fine weather; and if not hard, or knotted, or clearly marked off from a serene sky, does not often precede any important change.

Detached patches of cirrus, like little masses of wool or knotted feathers, in a clear sky, and of unusual figure, moving at more than the average rate, precede disturbances of great magnitude. The rays in straight lines are a good sign.
- [The last ten rules are by the Hon. F. A. R. Russell.]

Detached

Continued wet weather is attended by horizontal sheets of cirrus clouds, which subside quickly, passing into the cirro-stratus.

Indicating wet

When cirri merge into cirri-strati, and when cumuli increase towards evening and become lower, expect wet weather.

Streaky clouds across the wind foreshow rain.
- Scotland.

If cirrus clouds form in fine weather with a falling barometer, it is almost sure to rain. - Howard.

These clouds announce the east wind. If their under surface is level, and their streaks pointing upwards, they indicate rain; if downwards, wind and dry weather.
- Howard.

Rain and wind

If the cirrus clouds get lower and denser to leeward, it presages bad weather from the opposite quarter.

Bad weather

The cirrus clouds are the swiftest of all, moving at an average speed of seventy-eight miles an hour.
- Clayton.

Speed

METEOROLOGY. PLATE 4

CYCLONES AND ANTICYCLONES

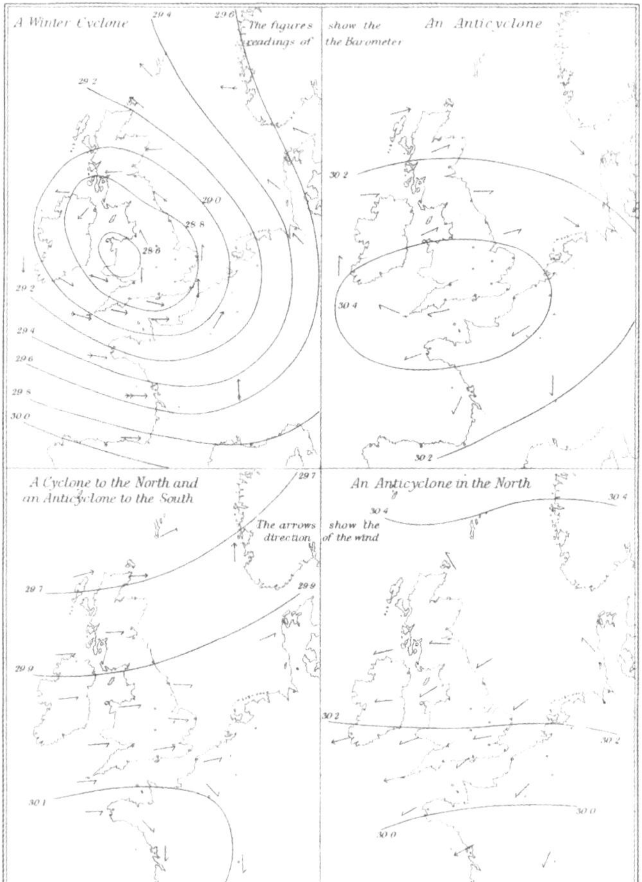

RULES FOR WEATHER ACCORDING TO THE DIRECTION OF MOTION OF CIRRUS CLOUDS.

"Cirrus moving from north or north-east with a high barometer is a sign of settled weather in summer, and of temporarily fine weather in winter; with a low barometer, it is a sign of marked improvement in the weather.

Moving from east - a rare occurrence - is a sign of fine weather in winter, but of unsettled weather in summer. Cirrus moving from south-east (but it rarely does so with a low and unsteady barometer) is a sign of improving weather in winter, and in summer frequently indicates coming thunderstorms.

Moving from south generally indicates unsettled weather, especially in summer.

Moving from south-west indicates unsettled, and sometimes stormy, weather in winter. In summer it often precedes thunderstorms; but with a high barometric pressure and a high temperature it frequently has no disturbing influence, and is then usually replaced by cirro-macula (speckle cloud). Cirrus from west is commonly in summer a symptom of fair weather, but it is less so in winter.

Cirrus from north-west, when not tending to the form cirro-filum (thread-like cirrus), is an indication of temporary fine weather, especially in summer."
- Rev. Clement Ley (Cloudland).

V-POINT, OR POINT OF CONVEYANCE, FOR THE FIBRES OF CIRRO-FILUM (thread-like cirrus).

1. A V-point north commonly indicates improving weather over and to the south, but distant atmospheric disturbances in the north and north-west.

2. A V-point north-east, temporarily settled weather, especially with high barometer.

3. A V-point east, settled weather in winter; in summer, with high temperature, it sometimes indicates disturbances, which will be felt most to the south-west of the place of observation.

4. A V-point south-east, fine weather in winter, except when occurring immediately after heavy rain, when it is commonly followed by squalls. In summer it is almost invariably followed by thunder, with damp and sultry weather.

5. A V-point south with fairly low barometer, after a fall of rain, indicates showery weather in summer, and rough, squally weather in winter, with south-west or west winds, especially if the cloud velocity is great. With a high barometer, it indicates in summer thunderstorms from south-west, but in winter may be taken as a sign of favourable weather.

6. A V-point south-west, moderately fine weather.

7. A V-point west, fine weather in the warm months. The weather to the south and south-east of the observer is then usually dry and warm, but to the extreme north-west unsettled. In winter it is a symptom of unsettled weather.

8. A V-point north-west is bad; when it occurs just after a rise in the barometer, it indicates a sudden fall, with wind and rain. A V-point between west-north-west and north-west, especially with rapid cloud movement, is always followed by unsettled weather.

Speckle cloud

Cirro-macula (speckle-cloud) nearly always occurs in warm weather, when the atmosphere at the earth's surface has but little lateral motion.
- Rev. Clement Ley (Cloudland).

Storms	When the cirrus clouds appear at lower elevations than usual, and with a denser character, expect a storm from the opposite quarter to the clouds.
Pointing upwards	When streamers point upward, the clouds are falling, and rain is at hand; when streamers point downwards, the clouds are ascending, and drought is at hand.
Streaky	When after a clear frost long streaks of cirrus are seen with their ends bending towards each other as they recede from the zenith, and when they point to the north-east, a thaw and a south-west wind may be expected.
Barred	The barred or ribbed cirrus is considered by the Hon. F. A. R. Russell as good a danger-signal as that given by a falling barometer.
Weather-head cirrus	In Shetland the name of 'weather-head' is given to a band of cirrus passing through the zenith; and they say if it lies north-east to south-west, good weather comes; but if south-east to north-west, a gale is looked for.
	After a drought or a spell of fine weather, when mares' tails are seen running across the sky, followed next day at about the same hour by alto-cumulus, then rain will follow within twelve hours. - Col. H. M. Saunders, of Cheltenham.
	If in fair weather a thin cloud appears stretched at length and feathery, the winter will not end yet. - Theophrastus ("Signs, etc." J. G. Wood's Translation).

Horizontal or slightly inclined masses, attenuated towards a part or the whole of their circumference, bent downwards, or undulated, separate, or in groups, or consisting of small clouds having these characters. - Howard.

CIRRO-STRATUS
Definition

Cirro-stratus clouds, according to the observation of Mr. John Aitken, are always in a decaying or diminishing condition.
- Nature (June 18, 1896).

Wind

If clouds look as if scratched by a hen,
Get ready to reef your topsails then.
- Nautical.

Hen's scarts [scratchings] and filly tails
Make lofty ships carry low sails.

One of the surest signs of rain with which I am acquainted is that of the sky assuming an almost colourless appearance in the direction of the wind, especially if lines of dark or muddy cirro-strati lie above and about the horizon, and the milkiness gradually become muddy. - E. J. Lowe.

Hairy

Comoid cirri, or cirri in detached tufts, called "mares's tails," may be regarded as a sign of wind, which follows, often blowing from the quarter to which the fibrous tails have previously pointed.
- T. Forster.

Trace in the sky the painter's brush,
Then winds around you soon will rush.

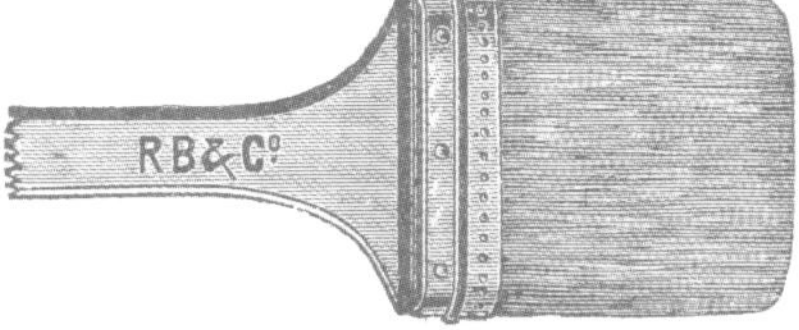

The cloud called "goat's hair" or the "gray mare's tail" forebodes wind.

The form of cloud popularly called "Noah's ark" is also called the "magnetic cirrus," and is said to consist of fine ice crystals, and to be accompanied by magnetic disturbances.

Ark-like

A long stripe of cloud, sometimes called a salmon, sometimes a Noah's ark, when it stretches east and west, is a sign of a storm; but when north and south, of fine weather.

This is called in the Yorkshire dales "Noaship," and the old Danes called it "Nolskeppet."
- Dr. J. C. Atkinson (Forty Years in a Moorland Parish).

"When looking in a westerly or easterly direction, if the centre of the bank of cirro-velum is to the right of the point from which the edge, or the cirro-filum outside the edge, is moving the probability of bad weather is not nearly so great as if this centre

was to the left of this point. But looking in a northerly or southerly direction, if the centre lies to the right of the direction of motion of the edge of the bank, the ensuing weather will be worse than if it lies to the left."
- Rev. Clement Ley ("Cloudland").

Cloud ship

In the Eifel district of the Lower Rhine they say, when the "cloud ship" turns its head to the south, rain will soon follow.

Wane cloud

When a plain sheet of the wane cloud is spread over a large surface at eventide, or when the sky gradually thickens with this cloud, a fall of steady rain is usually the consequence.
- T. Forster.

Direction

In low pressure areas the stripes lie parallel to the isobars (lines of equal barometric pressure), while in high pressure areas the stripes cross the isobars at right angles. - Hildebrandsson.

Gloomy

Continuous cirrostrati gathering into unbroken gloom, and also the cloud called "goat's hair," or the "gray mare's tail," presage wind.
- Scotland.

Indicating wind

When after a shower the cirrostrati open up at the zenith, leaving broken or ragged edges pointing upwards, and settle down gloomily and compactly on the horizon, wind will follow, and will last for some time. - Scotland.

The cirro-stratus precedes winds and rains, and the approach of foul weather may sometimes be inferred from its greater or less abundance, and the permanent character it puts on.

Wind and rain

If clouds appear high in air in their white trains, wind, and probably rain, will follow.

When ash-coloured masses of cumulo-stratus and cirro-stratus cloud collect over the sea, extending in a line from south-east to south-west, expect rain, and probably wind, on the second day.
- C. L. Prince.

If long lines of cirrostrati extend along the horizon, and are slightly contracted in their centre, expect heavy rain the following day.
- C. L. Prince.

Rain

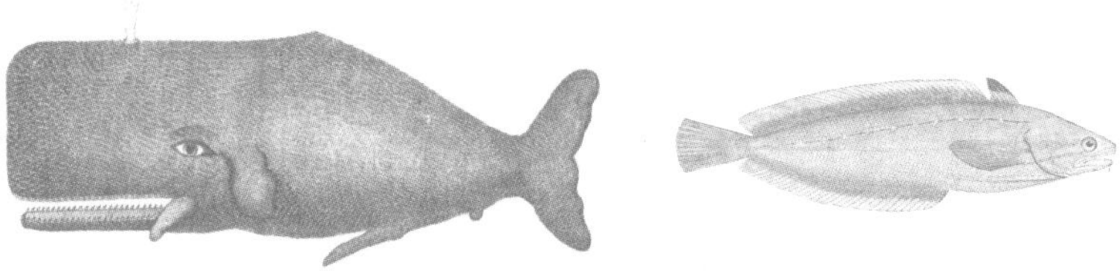

The cirro-stratus is doubtless the one alluded to by Polonius in "Hamlet" as "very like a whale."

Fish-shaped

The fish (hake) shaped cloud, if pointing east and west, indicates rain; if north and south, more fine weather.
- Bedfordshire.

North and south, the sign of drought;
East and west, the sign of blast.

With cirrus

Light, fleecy clouds in rapid motion, below compact, dark cirro-strati, foretell rain near at hand.
- Scotland.

Indicating thunder

The waved cirro-stratus indicates heat and thunder.

CIRRO-CUMULUS

Definition

Small, well-defined, roundish masses increasing from below. - Howard.

The average speed of cirro-cumulus clouds is seventy-one miles an hour.
- Clayton.

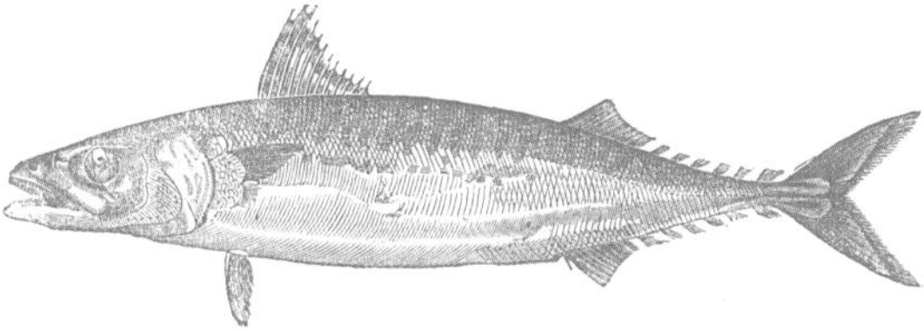

Indicating wind

Commonly called "mackerel sky."

Rain

Mackerel sky and mares' tails
Make lofty ships carry low sails.

Change

A mackerel sky denotes fair weather for that day, but rain a day or two after.

Mackerel sky, mackerel sky,
Never long wet and never long dry.

Mackerel clouds in sky,
Expect more wet than dry.

Mackerel scales,
Furl your sails.

If small white clouds are seen to collect together, their edges appearing rough, expect wind.

Before thunder, cirro-cumulus clouds often appear in very dense and compact masses, in close contact.

Indicating thunder

A curdly sky will not leave the earth long dry.

Curdled

When cirro-cumuli appear in winter, expect warm and wet weather. When cirri threads are brushed back from a southerly direction, expect rain and wind.

Direction

Small floating clouds over a bank of clouds, sign of rain.

Small

Wandering

In summer we apprehend a future storm when we see little black, loose clouds lower than the rest, wandering to and fro when at sunrise we see several clouds gather in the west; and, on the other hand, if these clouds disperse, it speaks fair weather.
- Ozanam.

Scattered

Fleecy clouds scattered over the sky denote storms; but clouds which rest upon one another like scales or tiles portend dry and fine weather.
- Bacon.

Dappled

A sky dappled with light clouds of the cirro-cumulus form in the early morning generally leads to a fine and warm day.
- Jenyns.

Dappled sky is not for long.
- France.

If woolly fleeces spread the heavenly way,
Be sure no rain disturbs the summer day.

A blue and white sky,
Never four-and-twenty hours dry.
- Northamptonshire.

A dappled sky,
like a painted woman,
soon changes its face.
- France.

Crowded

Small white clouds,
like a flock of sheep,
driving north-west,
indicate continued fine weather.

If clouds appear like a flock of sheep, and red in colour, wind follows.

The Germans call the white, fleecy cirro-cumulus clouds "heaven's lambs."

Storm

The cirro-cumulus, when accompanied by the cumulo-stratus, is a sure indication of a coming storm.

Storm	There is an intermediate form of sad-coloured cloud between cirro-stratus and cirro-cumulus, and which resembles waves seemingly equi-distant from each other, which is a sure indication of thunder. - Basil Woodd Smith.
Outlines	If soft and delicate in outline, it may be followed by a continuance of fine weather; but if dense, abundant, and associated with cirrus, it signifies electrical disturbance and change of wind, often resulting in thunderstorms in summer or gales in winter.
High	High cirro-cumulus commonly appears a few hours or days before thunderstorms. It generally moves with the prevailing surface wind. The harder and more definite the outline, the more unsettled the coming weather. In winter clearly marked, high cirro-cumulus is a sign of bad weather. If the cloud be continuous in long streaks, dense, and with rounded, knobby outlines, stormy weather follows generally within two or three days.
Soft	When cirro-cumulus is seen overhead, if the fleeces gently merge into each other, and the edges are soft and transparent, settled weather prevails; and if the middle part of the fleeces look shadowy, so much the better.
Slow	Cirro-cumulus at a great height and in large masses, moving slowly from north-east, is a sign of the continuance of the wind in that quarter. - Hon. F. A. R. Russell.

CUMULUS

Definition

Convex or conical heaps increasing upwards from a horizontal base.
- Howard.

Rainballs

Cumulus clouds are called rainballs in Lancashire.

Udders

Pendulous cumuli are compared in the Vedic hymns to the udders of the cows of Indra.

Stormy

In India, if a cumulus cloud have a stratum of flat cloud above it, a coming storm is indicated.

Piled up

Sometimes the clouds appear to be piled in several tiers or stories, one above the other (Gilbert, "Phys". iv. 1, declares that he has sometimes seen and observed five together), whereof the lowest are always the blackest, though it sometimes appears otherwise, as the whiter most attract the sight. Two stories, if thick, portend instant rain (especially if the lower one appear overcharged); many tiers denote a three days' rain.
- Bacon.

Fleecy

Refreshing showers or heavier rains are near
When piled in fleecy heaps the clouds appear.
- Aratus (J. Lamb).

Dark

If a black cloud eclipse the solar ray,
And sudden night usurp the place of day.
(Indicating rain.)
- Aratus (J. Lamb).

Opening and closing

If clouds open and close, rain will continue.

Round-topped

A round-topped cloud, with flattened base,
Carries rainfall in its face.

White

A white loaded cloud, called by the ancients a white tempest, is followed in summer by showers of very small hail, in winter by snow. - Bacon.

Wind

Cumulus clouds high up are said to show that south and south-west winds are near at hand; and stratified clouds low down, that east or north winds will prevail. - Scotland.

Tower-like indicating rain

Large irregular masses of cloud, "like rocks and towers," are indicative of showery weather. If the barometer be low, rain is all the more probable. - Jenyns.

When clouds appear like rocks and towers,
The earth's refreshed by frequent showers.

When mountains and cliffs in the clouds appear,
Some sudden and violent showers are near.

In the morning mountains,
In the evening fountains.
- Herbert.

When the clouds rise in terraces of white, soon will the country of the corn priests be pierced with the arrows of rain. - Zuñi Indians.

If during a storm, with the north wind blowing, a white under-light appear from the north, but on the south a cumulus cloud is extended opposite to it, it generally indicates a change to fair weather.
- Theophrastus ("Signs, etc." J. G. Wood's Translation).

Augmenting

Before rain these clouds augment in volume with great rapidity, sink to a lower elevation, and become fleecy and irregular in appearance, with their surfaces full of protuberances. They usually also remain stationary, or else sail against the surface wind previous to wet weather.

Banking up

When the clouds bank up the contrary way to the wind, there will be rain.

If on a fair day in winter a white bank of clouds arise in the south, expect snow.

Water-waggons

The rounded clouds called "water-waggons" which fly alone in the lower currents of wind forebode rain. - T. Forster.

Diminishing

When the cumulus clouds are smaller at sunset than they were at noon, expect fair weather.

Wet calm

The formation of cumulus clouds to leeward during a strong wind indicates the approach of a calm with rain.

Indicating hail, snow, or rain

If clouds are formed like fleeces, deep and dense, or thick and close towards the middle, the edges being very white, while the surrounding sky is bright and blue, they are of a frosty coldness, and will speedily fall in hail, snow, or rain.

Storm

And another storm brewing; I hear it sing i' the wind. Yond' same black cloud, yond' huge one, looks like a foul bumbard that would shed his liquor... Yond' same cloud cannot chuse but fall by pailfuls. - Shakespeare ("Tempest").

The pocky* cloud or heavy cumulus, looking like festoons of drapery, forebodes a storm. - Scotland.

Thunder

In summer or harvest, when the wind has been south for two or three days, and it grows very hot, and you see clouds rise with great white tops like towers, as if one were upon the top of another, and joined together with black on the nether side, there will be thunder and rain suddenly. If two such clouds arise, one on

* Pock, a bag

either hand, it is time to make haste to shelter.
- Shepherd of Banbury.

When cumulus clouds become heaped up to leeward during a strong wind at sunset, thunder may be expected during the night.

Changing

Well-defined cumuli, forming a few hours after sunrise, increasing towards the middle of the day, and decreasing towards evening, are indicative of settled weather: if instead of subsiding in the evening and leaving the sky clear they keep increasing, they are indicative of wet. - Jenyns.

CUMULO-STRATUS

Definition

The cirro-stratus blended with the cumulus, and either appearing intermixed with the heaps of the latter, or superadding a widespread structure to its base.
- Howard.

Collecting

When large masses of cumulo-strati cloud collect simultaneously in the north-east and south-west, with the wind east, expect cold rain or snow in the course of a few hours. The wind will ultimately back to north.
- C. L. Prince.

On horizon

When at sea, if the cumulo-stratus clouds appear on the horizon, it is a sign that the weather is going to break up.

Tails or feathers

If there be long points, tails, or feathers hanging from the thunder or rain clouds, five or six or more degrees above the horizon, with little wind in summer, thunder may be expected, but the storm will be of short duration.

Streak	A horizontal streak or band of clouds immediately in front of the mountains on the east side of Salt Lake Valley is an indication of rain within one or two days. When black clouds cover the western horizon, rain will follow soon, and extend to the eastward over the valley. - United States.
Striped	If long strips of clouds drive at a slow rate high in air, and gradually become larger, the sky having been previously clear, expect rain.
NIMBUS Definition	A rain cloud - a cloud or system of clouds from which rain is falling. It is a horizontal sheet over which the cirrus spreads, while the cumulus enters it laterally and from beneath. - Howard.
Prophet clouds	When scattered patches or streaks of nimbus come driving up from the south-west, they are called by the sailors "prophet clouds," and indicate wind.
Bells	Hark! from the little village below us, the bells of the church are ringing for rain! Priests and peasants in long procession come forth and kneel on the arid plain. They have not long to wait, for I see in the south uprising a little cloud, That before the sun shall be set will cover the sky above us as with a shroud. - Longfellow ("Golden Legend").
Storm	If a little cloud suddenly appear in a clear sky, especially if it come from the west, or somewhere in the south, there is a storm brewing. - Bacon.

See we not hanging in the clouds each hour
So many seas, still threat'ning down to pour,
Supported only by th' aire's agitation,
Selfly too weak for the least weight's foundation.
- Du Bartas ("Divine Weekes").

STRATUS
Definition

A widely extended, continuous, horizontal sheet, increasing from below. - Howard.

Fine

These clouds have always been regarded as the harbingers of fine weather, and there are few finer days in the year than when the morning breaks out through a disappearing stratus cloud.

Night

A stratus at night, with a generally diffused fog the next morning, is usually followed by a fine day, if the barometer be high and steady. If the barometer keep rising, the fog may last all day; if the barometer be low, the fog will probably turn to rain. - Jenyns.

On mountains

When mountains extend north and south, if fog or mist comes from the west, expect fair weather.
If mist comes from the top of mountains, expect rain in summer, snow in winter.
- Apache Indians.

Fair weather

Thin, white, fleecy, broken mist, slowly ascending the sides of a mountain whose top is uncovered, predicts a fair day.
- Scotland.

A few parallel streaks of cloud, seldom more than three or four in number, appearing either as white streaks on the blue or, more rarely, as darker streaks against nimbus or cumulo-nimbus, are a sure prognostic of thunder.
- B. Woodd Smith ("Nature", June 18, 1896).

This is no pilgrim's morning - yon grey mist lies upon hill and dale and field and forest.
- Sir W. Scott ("Pirate").

Storm

Oh! The morning mist lies heavy upon yonder chain of isles, nor has it permitted us since daybreak even a single glimpse of Fitful Head.
(Indicating approaching storm.)
- Sir W. Scott ("Pirate", ch. iv.).

On hills

If mist rise to the hilltops and there stay, expect rain shortly.

When the mist comes from the hill,
Then good weather it doth spill;
When the mist comes from the sea.
Then good weather it will be.
When the mist creeps up the hill,
Fisher, out and try your skill;
When the mist begins to nod,
Fisher, then put past your rod.
- Kirkcudbright.

Rising and falling

Misty clouds, forming or hanging on heights, show wind and rain coming, if they remain, increase, or descend. If they rise or disperse, the weather will improve.
- Fitzroy.

Clouds upon hills, if rising,
do not bring rain;
if falling, rain follows.

Thick When the clouds on the hilltops are thick and in motion, rain to the south-west is regarded as certain to follow. - Scotland.

Small When it gangs up i' fops,*
It'll fa' down i' drops.
- North Country.

Hanging When mountains and hills appear capped by clouds that hang about and embrace them, storms are imminent. - Bacon.

Ascending When the clouds go up the hill,
They'll send down water to turn a mill.
- Hampshire.

Hymettus If during the winter there is
a long cloud over Hymettus,
it indicates a prolongation of the winter.

* Small clouds on hills.

Athos, Olympus and the peaks of mountains generally, if covered by cloud, indicate a storm.
- Theophrastus ("*Signs, etc.*" J. G. Wood's Translation).

When Olympus, Athos, and generally all hills that give indications, have their tops clear, it indicates fair weather.
- Theophrastus ("*Signs, etc.*" J. G. Wood's Translation).

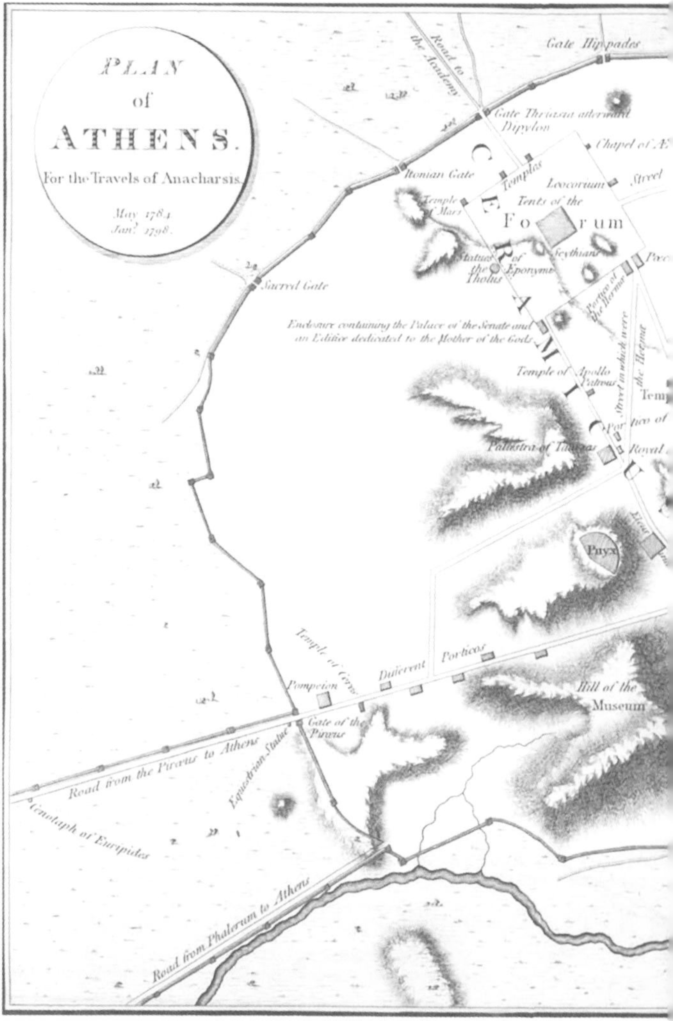
PLAN
of
ATHENS.
For the Travels of Anacharsis.
Gate Hippades
Road to the Academy
Dipylon
Itonian Gate
Temples
Leocorium
Street
Temple of Mars
Tents of the
Scythians
Forum
Statues of the Eponyms
the Tholus
Sacred Gate
Enclosure containing the Palace of the Senate and an Edifice dedicated to the Mother of the Gods
Portico of the Hermæ
Street in which were the Hermæ
Temple of Apollo Patrous
Palæstra of Taureas
Pnyx
Temple of Ceres
Pompeion
Different Porticos
Hill of the Museum
Gate of the Piræus
Equestrian Statue
Road from the Piræus to Athens
Cenotaph of Euripides
Road from Phalerum to Athens

Gate of Melite
Street leading to Gate
House of Phocion
MOUNT ANCHESMUS
Gym-nasium
Gate Diomeia
Temple and Gardens of Venus
Prytaneum
Chapel of Agraulus
Street of the Tripods
Gate Diocharis
Gym-nasium
CITADEL
Temple of Minerva
Odeum
Theatre of Bacchus
Ancient Temple of Bacchus of the Marshes
DROMOS
LIMNÆ
or the Marshes
Gate of Ægeus
Altar of Orithya
Temple of Diana Agrotera
Temple of Ceres
AGRÆ
MOUNT HYMETTUS
ILISSUS R.
English Yards.
200 400 600 800 1000 1200
Olympian Stadia.
1 2 3 4 5 6
French Toises.
50 100 200 300 400 500 600

If the lesser Hymettus (which is called Dry) has a small cloud in its hollow, it is a sign of rain; and if the Great Hymettus in summer has white clouds above and on its side it is a sign of rain.
So also if Dry Hymettus has white clouds above and on its side.
[The Hymettus (Greater and Less) Hills, about five miles Southeast of Athens.]
- Theophrastus ("Signs, etc." J. G. Woods Translation).

Whenever a long white cloud envelops Hymettus downwards from its peaks at night, rain occurs, as a rule, within a few days.
- Theophrastus ("Signs, etc." J. G. Wood's Translation).

See, Glaucus! The deep sea already is surging with waves; and around the tops of the hills an upright cloud stands encircling them-the sign of a storm.
- Archilochus (quoted by Theophrastus: "Signs, etc." J. G. Wood's Translation).

In whatever direction a cloud stretches out from the peak of a mountain, in that direction will the wind blow.
- Theophrastus ("Signs, etc." J. G. Wood's Translation).

Whenever the clouds girt the mountains quite down to the sea, it is a sign of fair weather.
- Theophrastus ("Signs, etc." J. G. Wood's Translation).

If clouds settle down on the back of a mountain, the wind will blow from behind it also.
- Theophrastus ("Signs, etc." J. G. Wood's Translation).

Pendle's Head

When the Pendle's Head is free from clouds, the people thereabout expect a halcyon day, and those on the banks of the Can (or Kent) in Westmoreland can tell what weather to look for from the voice of its falls.

For when they to the north the noise do easiest hear,
They constantly aver the weather will be clear.
And when they to the south, again they boldly say
It will be clouds or rain the next approaching day.
- Drayton ("Polyolbion").

South Downs

When the South Downs look blue and near after heavy rain, a gale may be expected within thirty hours. When on a cloudless summer day you perceive a white flocculent mist lying upon the summit of the South Downs (i.e. from Mount Harry to Lewes Racecourse), expect very hot weather within three days. - C. L. Prince.

Bell Rock — Clouds on Bell Rock Light
mean rain at Arbroath.

Firle Head — When Firle Hill and Long Man has a cap,
We at A'ston gets a drap. - Sussex.

Wolsonbury — When Wolsonbury has a cap,
Hurstpierpoint will have a drap.
- Sussex.

Ross — Clouds on Ross-shire Hills mean rain at Ardersier, on the south-east of the Moray Frith.

Cocking — A curious phenomenon is observable in the neighbourhood of Cocking, West Sussex. From the leafy recesses of the hangers of beech on the escarpments of the downs, there rises in unsettled weather a mist which rolls among the trees like the smoke out of a chimney. This exhalation is called

"foxes-brewings," whatever that may mean, and if it tends westward towards Cocking, rain follows speedily. Hence the local proverb:

> "When Foxes-brewings go to Cocking,
> Foxes-brewings come back dropping."
> - Lower ("History of Sussex").

Clouds on Orkney Isles
mean rain at Cape Wrath.

Orkney

Clouds on Kilpatrick Hills mean rain at Eaglesham, in Renfrewshire.

Kilpatrick Hills

Clouds on Ailsa Craig mean rain at Cumbrae.

Ailsa Craig

Sailors say it is a sign of bad weather when the "tablecloth" (a cloud so called) is spread on Table Mountain.

Cape Town

Bever

If Bever hath a cap,
You churls of the vale look to that.
- Leicestershire.

Ladie Lift

When Ladie Lift*
Puts on her shift,
She feares a downright raine;
But when she doffs it, you will finde
The raine is o'er, and still the winde,
And Phœbus shine againe. - Herefordshire.

Skiddaw

If Skiddaw hath a hat,
Scruffel wots full well of that. - Cumberland.

When Skiddaw hath a cap,
Criffel wots fu' well of that.
Heavy clouds on Skiddaw, especially with a south wind, the farmer of Kirkpatrick Fleming looks on as an indication of coming rain.
[Note. - Skiddaw lies to the south of the place.]

* A clump of trees near Weobley

When Moncayo and Guara have their white caps on,
It is good for Castile and better for Aragon. - Spain.

Moncayo

When Traprain puts on his hat,
The Lothian lads may look to that.
- Haddingtonshire.

Traprain

When Ruberslaw puts on his cowl,
The Dunion on his hood,
Then a' the wives of Teviotside
Ken there will be a flood.
- Roxburghshire.

Ruberslaw

[Also said of Craigowl and Collie Law in Forfarshire, substituting "Lundy lads" for "the wives of Teviotside." - Robert Chambers.]

Craigowl and Collie Law

When Falkland Hill puts on his cap,
The Howe o' Fife will get a drap;
And when the Bishop draws his cowl,
Lookout for wind and weather foul.

Falkland Hill, Lomond Range

When Cheviot ye see put on his cap,
Of rain ye'll have a wee bit drap.
- Scotland.

Cheviot

When Largo Law puts on his hat,
Let Kellie Law beware of that;
When Kellie Law gets on his cap,
Largo Law may laugh at that.
- Scotland.
[Note. - Largo Law is to the south-west of Kellie Law.]

Largo Law

Scotch Hills

A cloud on Sidlaw Hills foretells rain to Carmylie.
A cloud on Bin Hill foretells rain to Cullen.
A cloud on Paps of Jura foretells rain to Gigha.
A cloud on Mull of Kintyre foretells rain to Cara.

Cairnsmore

When Cairnsmore wears a hat,
The Macher's Rills may laugh at that.
[Note. - Cairnsmore is north-north-east of Macher's Rills, Wigtownshire, Scotland.]

When Cairnsmuir puts on his hat,
Palmuir and Skyreburn laugh at that.
[Note. - Palmuir and Skyreburn are rivulets which rise rapidly whenever rain falls about Cairnsmuir.]

When Criffel wears a hat
Skiddaw wots full we o' that.

Criffel

If Corsancone put on his cap, and the Knipe be clear, it will rain within twenty-four hours.
[Note. - This is a sign which it is said never fails. Corsancone Hill is to the East and the Knipe to the south-west of the New Cumnock districts, where the proverb is current.]

Corsancone

The rolling of clouds landward and their gathering about the summit of Criffel is regarded as a sign of foul weather in Dumfries and Kirkpatrick Fleming, and intervening parishes.
[Note. - Criffel is to the Southwest of the place.]

Criffel

Craighill

There is a high wooded hill above Lochnaw Castle;
Take care when Lady Craighill puts on her mantle.
The Lady looks high and knows what is coming;
Delay not one moment to get under covering.
[Note. - The hill lies to the north-west of the district where this doggerel is quoted.]

Riving Pike

If Riving Pike do wear a hood,
Be sure the day will ne'er be good.
- Lancashire.

Helm cloud

A cloud, called the "helm cloud," or "helm bar," hovering about the hilltops for a day or two, is said to presage wind and rain. - Yorkshire.

Lookout

When Lookout Mountain has its cap on,
it will rain in six hours. - United States

Mists

Spring	If mists occur after the vernal equinox, they indicate airs and winds till the sixth month thereafter. - Theophrastus ("Signs, etc." J. G. Wood's Translation).
Disappearing	If mists and fogs ascend and return upwards, they denote rain; and if this take place suddenly, so that they appear to be sucked up, they foretell winds; but if they fall and rest in the valleys, it will be fine weather. - Bacon.
Vapours and winds	Wherever there is a plentiful generation of vapours, and that at certain times, you may be sure that at those times periodical winds will arise. - Bacon.
White	White mist in winter indicates frost. - Scotland.
Black	Black mist indicates coming rain.
Mist and rain	Mists above, water below. - Spain.
In low ground	If mists rise in low ground and soon vanish, expect fair weather. - Shepherd of Banbury.

A white mist in the evening, over a meadow with a river, will be drawn up by the sun next morning, and the day will be bright. Five or six fogs successively drawn up portend rain.

River

Where there are high hills, and the mist which hangs over the lower lands draws towards the hills in the morning, and rolls up to the top, it will be fair; but if the mist hangs upon the hills, and drags along the woods, there will be rain.
- Rev. W. Jones.

Rising

In the evenings of autumn and spring, vapour arising from a river is regarded as a sure indication of coming frost. - Scotland.

A northern harr (mist)
Brings weather from far.

Northern

Mists dispersing on the plain
Scatter away the clouds and rain;
But when they rise to the mountain-tops,
They'll soon descend in copious drops.

Spreading

Three foggy or misty mornings indicate rain.
- Oregon.

Misty morning

S
A
B
C

Haze

Haze and western sky purple indicate fair weather. Indications

Hazy weather is thought to prognosticate frost in winter, snow in spring, fair weather in summer, and rain in autumn.
- Scotland.

A sudden haze coming over the atmosphere is due to the mixing of two currents of unequal temperatures: it may end in rain, or in an increase of temperature; or it may be the precursor of a change, though not immediate. - Jenyns.

4

Dew

The dews of the evening industriously shun;
They're the tears of the sky for the loss of the sun.

Evening

If the dew lies plentifully on the grass after a fair day, it is a sign of another.

If not, and there is no wind, rain must follow.
- Rev. W. Jones.

Dew and fog

When in the morning the dew is heavy and remains long on the grass, when the fog in the valleys is slowly dispersed and lingers on the hillsides, when the clouds seem to be taking a higher place, and when a few loose cirro-strati float gently along, serene weather may be expected for the greater part of that day.
- Scotland.

Night

If in clear summer nights there is no dew, expect rain next day.
- C. L. Prince.

Fine weather

Dew is an indication of fine weather; so is fog.
- Fitzroy.

Calm

Dew is produced in serene weather and in calm places.
- Aristotle.

Dispersing	If the dew is evaporated immediately upon the sun rising, rain and storm follow in the afternoon; but if it stays and glitters for a long time after sunrise, the day continues fair. De Quincey's "Note to Analects from Richter."
Profuse	If there is a profuse dew in summer, it is about seven to one that the weather will be fine. - E. J. Lowe.
Evening	With dew before midnight, The next day will sure be bright.
South wind	During summer a heavy dew is sometimes followed by a southerly wind in the afternoon.
Heavy	If there is a heavy dew, it indicates fair weather; no dew, it indicates rain.
Rain	If nights three dewless there be, 'Twill rain you're sure to see.
Mountain	When the dew is seen shining on the leaves, the mist rolled down from the mountain last night. - Zuñi Indians.
No dew	When there is no dew at such times as usually there is, it foreshoweth rain. - Wing, 1649.

Fog

Falling	When the fog falls, fair weather follows; when it rises, rain ensues.
August	In the Mississippi valley, when fogs occur in August, expect fever and ague in the following fall.
Damp	If there be a damp fog or mist, accompanied by wind, expect rain.
Light	Light fog passing under sun from south to north in the morning indicates rain in twenty-four or forty-eight hours.
With frost	If there be continued fog, expect frost. - United States.

When the fog goes up the mountain, you may go hunting; when it comes down the mountain, you may go fishing. In the former case it will be fair, in the latter it will rain.

Hunting

Change — Fogs are signs of a change.

Winter — Heavy fog in winter, when it hangs below trees, is followed by rain.

Sea and hills

A fog from the sea
Brings honey to the bee;
A fog from the hills
Brings corn to the mills.
- Pembrokeshire.

Fog from seaward, fair weather;
fog from landward, rain.
- New England.

Sea

When with hanging fog smoke rises vertically,
rain follows.

Hanging

Whenever there is a fog, there is little or no rain.
- Theophrastus ("Signs, etc." J. G. Wood's Translation).

Fog is caused by a white bear
drinking too much water and bursting.
During fog, bears come out.
- Labrador.

Superstition

Rain

When God wills, it rains with any wind. - Spain. Wind

Some rain, some rest;
Fine weather isn't always best.

No one so surely pays his debt
As wet to dry and dry to wet.
- Wiltshire.

Changes

Rain, rain pouring
Sets the bulls a-roaring. - Suffolk.

Pouring

With the rain of the north-east comes the ice fruit [hail].
- Zuñi Indians.

North-east

Rain from the north-east in Germany continues
three days.

Rain from the east,
Two days at least.

East

Rain from the south prevents the drought;
But rain from the west is always best.

South

Rain which sets in with a south wind on the north
Pacific coast will probably last.

If it begin to rain from the south, with a high wind, for two or three hours, and the wind falls, but the rain continues, it is likely to rain twelve hours or more, and does usually rain till a north wind clears the air. These long rains seldom hold above twelve hours, or happen above once a year.
- Shepherd of Banbury.

Rain with south or south-west thunder brings squalls on successive days.

West

When rain comes from the west, it will not last long.
- United States.

Short

The faster the rain, the quicker the hold up.
- Norfolk.

Long foretold

Rain long foretold, long last;
Short notice, soon past.

Mountains

Rain comes from a mass of vapour which is cooled.
- Aristotle.

Mountains cool the uplifted vapour, converting it again into water.
- Aristotle.

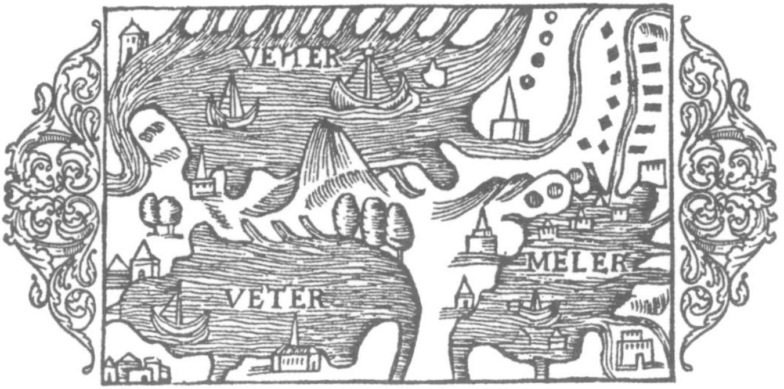

Small showers

Small showers last long,
but sudden storms are short.
- Shakespeare ("Richard II").

Morning

Rain before seven,
Lift before eleven.

If rain begins at early morning light,
'Twill end ere day at noon is bright.

Morning rains are soon past.
- France.

Rain afore church
Rain all the week, little or much.
- Norfolk.

Night

Night rains
Make drowned fens.
- East Anglia.

Custom

In Burmah the inhabitants have a custom of pulling a rope to produce rain. A rain party and a drought party tug against each other, the rain party being allowed the victory, which in the popular notion is generally followed by rain.
- Folk-Lore Journal,
vol. i. p. 214.

Night and morning

When it rains in the morning,
it will be fine at night.
- China.

Before sunrise

If it begin to rain an hour or two before sunrising, it is likely to be fair before noon, and so continue that day; but if the rain begin an hour after sunrising, it is likely to rain all that day, except the rainbow be seen before it rains.
- Shepherd of Banbury.

When it rains about the break of day,
The traveller's sorrows pass away.
- China.

Rain at daybreak

If the rain falls on the dew, it will fall all day.
- Bergamo.

Dew

A fall of small drizzling rain, especially in the morning, is a sure sign of wind to follow.
- Newhaven.

Drizzle

If it rain at midnight with a south wind, it will generally last above twelve hours.

Midnight

After rains, the wind most often blows in the places where the rain falls, and winds often cease when rain begins to fall.
- Aristotle.

Rain and wind

Five days' rain, ten days' wind, are both good omens.
- China.

A hasty shower of rain falling when the wind has raged some hours, soon allays it.
- Pointer.

Small rain abates high wind.
- France.

Marry the rain to the wind, and you have a calm.

Small

A small rain may allay a great storm.
- T. Fuller.

Sudden

Sudden rains never last long; but when the air grows thick by degrees, and the sun, moon, and stars shine dimmer and dimmer, then it is likely to rain six hours usually.
- Shepherd of Banbury.

From north or south

It is better both for plants and animals that rain from the north should precede that from the south, but it should be sweet and not salt to the taste.
- Theophrastus ("Signs, etc." J. G. Wood's Translation).

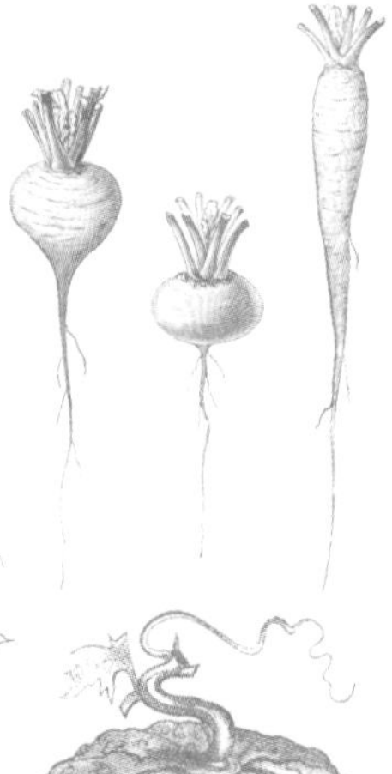

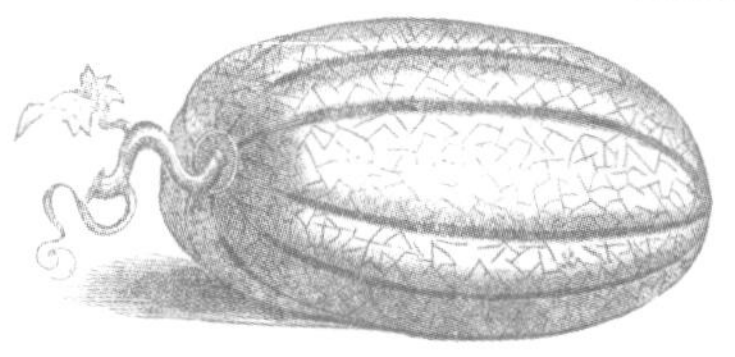

Sunshine

If it rains when the sun shines, it will rain the next day.

If it rains while the sun is shining,
the devil is beating his grandmother.
He is laughing, and she is crying.

After rain comes sunshine.

Sunshine and shower, rain again to-morrow.

If it rain when the sun shines, it will surely rain the next day about the same hour. - Suffolk.

A sunshiny shower
Never lasts half an hour. - Bedfordshire.

Bright rain
Makes fools fain [glad]. - Scotland.

Showers short

If short showers come during dry weather, they are said to "harden the drought" and indicate no change. - Scotland.

Preceded by fair weather

There is usually fair weather before a settled course of rain. - Fitzroy.

Rain and snow

A foot deep of rain
Will kill hay and grain;
But three feet of snow
Will make them come mo [more]. - Devonshire.

Followed by hail

If hail appear after a long course of rain, it is a sign of clearing up. - Scotland.

Drying

Wet continues if the ground dries up too soon.

Sowing

Who soweth in rain, he shall reap it with tears. - Tusser.

Watering

Though it rains, do not neglect to water. - Spain.

Drought

After great droughts come great rains. - Holland.

Causing bubbles

When the rain causes bubbles to rise in water it falls upon, the shower will last long.

Ague

The first and last rains bring the ague. - Spain.

Rainbows

The old Norsemen called the rainbow
"The bridge of the gods."
- C. Swainson.

East and west

A rainbow can only occur when the clouds containing or depositing the rain are opposite to the sun; and in the evening the rainbow is in the east, and in the morning in the west; and as our heavy rains in this climate are usually brought by the westerly wind, a rainbow in the west indicates that the bad weather is on the road, whereas the rainbow in the east proves that the rain in these clouds is passing from us.
- Sir Humphry Davy (in "Salmonia").

In cloud

When a rainbow is formed in an approaching cloud, expect a shower; but when in a receding cloud, fine weather.
- C. L. Prince.

In spring

A rainbow in spring indicates fair weather for twenty-four hours.

In wind's eye

When a rainbow appears in wind's eye, rain is sure to follow.

S'
S
S''

f
r
d
n
b

A dog in the morning,
Sailor, take warning;
A dog in the night
Is the sailor's delight.
[A sun-dog, in nautical language, is a small rainbow near the horizon. - Roper.]

Windward

Rainbow to windward, foul fall the day;
Rainbow to leeward, damp runs away.
- Nautical.

Fair and foul

If a rainbow appear in fair weather, foul will follow; but if a rainbow appear in foul weather, fair will follow.

Broken

Whenever you observe the rainbow to be broken in two or three places, or perhaps only half of it visible, expect rainy weather for two or three days.
- C. L. Prince.

Morning and evening

Rainbow in morning shows that shower is west of us, and that we shall probably get it. Rainbow in the evening shows that shower is east of us, and is passing off.
- United States.

A rainbow in the morn, put your hook in the corn;
A rainbow in the eve, put your hook in the sheave.
- Cornwall.

Weather Lore

A Collection of
Proverbs, Sayings & Rules
Concerning the Weather

Also in this series:

Volume I
Weather in General

Volume II
Sun, Moon & Stars
The Elements - Sky, Air, Sound, Heat

Volume IV
The Elements
Wind, Sea, Thunder & Lightning, Frost, Hail, Snow, Ice

Volume V
Flora & Fauna

Volume VI
Instruments of Measure

beginner's hindi script

rupert snell

For over 60 years, more than 40 million people have learnt over 750 subjects the **teach yourself** way, with impressive results.

be where you want to be
with **teach yourself**

For UK order enquiries: please contact Bookpoint Ltd, 130 Milton Park, Abingdon, Oxon OX14 4SB. Telephone: +44 (0) 1235 827720, Fax: +44 (0) 1235 400454. Lines are open 9.00–18.00, Monday to Saturday, with a 24-hour message answering service. You can also order through our website www.madaboutbooks.com

For USA order enquiries: please contact McGraw-Hill Customer Services, P.O. Box 545, Blacklick, OH 43004-0545, USA. Telephone: 1-800-722-4726. Fax: 1-614-755-5645.

For Canada order enquiries: please contact McGraw-Hill Ryerson Ltd, 300 Water St, Whitby, Ontario L1N 9B6, Canada. Telephone: 905 430 5000. Fax: 905 430 5020.

British Library Cataloguing in Publication Data: a catalogue entry for this title is available from The British Library.

Library of Congress Catalog Card Number: On file

First published in UK 2000 by Hodder Headline Ltd, 338 Euston Road, London, NW1 3BH.

First published in US 2000 by Contemporary Books, a Division of The McGraw Hill Companies, 1 Prudential Plaza, 130 East Randolph Street, Chicago, IL 60601 USA.

This edition published 2003.

Printed in Great Britain for Hodder & Stoughton Educational, a division of Hodder Headline Ltd, 338 Euston Road, London NW1 3BH by Cox & Wyman Ltd, Reading, Berkshire.

Impression number	10 9 8 7 6 5 4 3 2 1
Year	2007 2006 2005 2004 2003

Acknowledgements

I am grateful to Lucy Rosenstein, Christopher Shackle and Emma Back for their comments on an earlier draft of this book. My thanks also to Amrik Kalsi, Aishvarj Kumar, Sanjukta Ghosh, Navnidhi Kaur, Urvi Mukhopadhyay, and Nilanjan Sarkar, for supplying examples of handwritten Devanagari; and to Usha and Renuka Madan for the anecdote appearing in Appendix 1.

The Hindi font used here is 'Jaisalmer', designed for the Apple Macintosh by Professor K.E. Bryant of the University of British Columbia; the Roman font with Indic diacritical marks is 'Normyn', devised by Mr K.R. Norman of the University of Cambridge.

Books on Hindi by the same author

Teach Yourself Hindi (with Simon Weightman), revised edition, London, Hodder & Stoughton, 2000.

Hindi and Urdu since 1800: a Common Reader (with Christopher Shackle), London, School of Oriental and African Studies, 1990; also Delhi, Heritage, 1990.

The Hindi Classical Tradition: a Braj Bhāṣā Reader, London, School of Oriental and African Studies, 1991; also Delhi, Heritage, 1992.

CONTENTS

PREFACE

How to use this book

The Hindi script – called Devanagari – is a beautifully logical writing system. Its phonetic arrangement makes it quite easy to learn, and once you know the basic four dozen (or so) characters you will be well on your way to reading the signs, posters, notices, street names, signposts and advertisements that are part of the everyday scene in North India.

Beginner's Hindi Script introduces Devanagari in the traditional order. The characters are introduced one by one in phonetic groups, steadily building up your ability to read and write. The book also gives you some information on the cultural orientation of the language, explaining where Hindi belongs in the history of Indian languages, and showing where its words come from.

The book is intended for beginners who are starting to learn Hindi from scratch, and who need guidance in pronunciation as well as in reading and writing. But it can also be used by those who already know something of the spoken language – perhaps learned from family or from Hindi films – and who wish to add an ability to read and write.

To gain the most benefit from the book, treat it as a course and work through it from beginning to end. But if you are keen to begin learning the characters without delay, you can turn straight to Unit 3 and start copying out the hand-written examples. The basic syllabary of Devanagari is set out in a matrix on page 15, which will give you enough information to help you identify and read many simple words; if you are out and about in India, you might perhaps like to keep a photocopy of this table with you to help you interpret signboards, notices and place names. However you use the book, doing the exercises (and checking your answers against the key at the back of the book) is the best way of learning the script thoroughly. You will find instructions for the exercises on page 23.

The illustrations are mostly taken from 'public' uses of Hindi in advertisements, shop signs and so on. Most of the vocabulary appearing in these, and in the tabulated examples, is given in the Glossary; and translations of any text appearing in these illustrations are given in Appendix 5.

Signboards contain, among other things, a high proportion of English words (in Devanagari script), and this helps you to start learning the script before making inroads into the language itself. But if you would like to begin formulating simple Hindi sentences of your own, you will find some useful pointers in Unit 5.

Finally, a note on computers. Although you may feel tempted to practise your Hindi on a computer, you should not do so until you have developed a good clear handwriting of your own: copying out the characters and words by hand is the best way of becoming familiar with their forms. Only when you are confident of your handwriting skills should you experiment with typing on the computer. Many Devanagari fonts are now available for use on both PC and Macintosh, and some can be downloaded free of charge from the Internet; the situation is changing so rapidly that it is not possible for precise guidance to be given here. The Devanagari in this book is set in the Macintosh-based font 'Jaisalmer', as noted in the acknowledgements.

Linguistic map of India. The shaded area indicates states where Hindi predominates; official languages of the other states are shown in italics.

UNIT 1
Introducing Devanagari

The Devanagari script: its history and significance

Hindi is written in the script called 'Devanāgarī', apparently meaning '[script] of the city of the gods' – although the original implication of this name is unknown. Devanagari is also used for the ancient languages Sanskrit and Prakrit, the modern languages Marathi and Nepali, and some regional dialects. Its shorter name 'Nagari' is sometimes preferred in the Hindi-speaking world; and whether or not the literal meaning of *nāgarī* as 'urbane, sophisticated' (associated with the *nagar*, 'city') is really implied here, its use reflects the admiration this script deserves as a wonderfully complete and logical writing system. Fortunately for the beginner, the phonetic basis of Devanagari makes learning it an easy and enjoyable task. For all its antiquity, the script is described as *bāl-bodh*, 'comprehensible by children' – a good omen for the would-be reader!

An example of the script will show you how easy its basics are to grasp. The box below lists three common Indian food items: have a look at the transcribed characters, and then see what's on the menu – reading left to right (see foot of page).

ा	ग	द	न	ल	स
ā	*g*	*d*	*n*	*l*	*s*

दाल

साग

नान

[Answer: *dāl* 'lentils', *sāg* 'spinach, greens', *nān* 'bread']

Transliteration

In this book, Devanagari is introduced through a transliteration system that is standard in academic writing on South Asia; see the matrix on page 15. This system differs from the less scientific transliteration used in English-language writing on India: perhaps the most obvious differences are in showing the most common vowel in the language as 'a' rather than 'u', and in the marking of long vowels with a superscript line, the macron – thus *panjābī* rather than 'Punjabi'.

Languages and scripts in India

Sanskrit is an Indo-Aryan language – that is to say, it belongs to the 'Aryan' (or 'Indian') part of the Indo-European language family, and shares a common ultimate origin with Greek and Latin. Thus Hindi, which derives from Sanskrit, is a direct, if distant, relative of European languages, as is apparent in many close similarities between words; the Hindi for 'name' is *nām*, a 'tooth' is *dānt* (think of 'dentist'), and 'mother' is the comfortably maternal *mātā*. When you learn Hindi through English, you are not as far from home as you may have thought.

Devanagari is one of several scripts that have developed from Brāhmī, the ancient script whose earliest record is in the Prakrit inscriptions of the emperor Aśoka (3rd century BC). The origins of Brāhmī are still debated; Indian scholarship often attributes them to the still-undeciphered script of the Indus Valley inscriptions, but a Semitic prototype has also been proposed. The relatively late date of the appearance of writing in the history of ancient India shows how important the *spoken* word has always been in Indian civilisation: texts were traditionally transmitted orally from generation to generation, and the prodigious feats of memory that this process entailed are still to be found in contemporary India, where the memorising of texts – whether a devotional Hindi epic or a poem by Keats – is still commonplace and deeply impressive. The transmission of culture in the subcontinent did not rely primarily on writing until modern times, and it is only during the present century that literacy has become relatively widespread, with a national figure of some 52% being recorded in the 1991 census (the next census will be in 2001). In earlier centuries, the practice of writing was essentially for the keeping of accounts and records, and some scripts have been developed specifically for these purposes; an example is Kaithī, a Devanagari-like script whose name indicates its connection to the Kāyasth community of scribes. Although great strides in literacy have been made in all parts of India since Independence in 1947, the Hindi-speaking area still remains low in the literacy tables, and more than half the people who speak Hindi or one of its dialects cannot read or write it. By working through this book, you will increase the number of people literate in Hindi!

Fig 1: Indian shop signs are often illustrated with the products on sale, partly because of low literacy levels (see Appendix 5 for translations)

Indian scripts have a phonetic perfection and sophistication that sets them apart from most other writing systems in the world. Apart from the Roman and Urdu scripts, all the major Indian scripts derive from Brāhmī; but their separate evolution over the centuries has brought about great stylistic diversity, and someone who knows Devanagari cannot automatically read Bengali, Gujarati or Panjabi even although their scripts follow the same principles. An example of regional specialisation is found in the South Indian scripts, where the early use of palm-leaf as a writing material led to the development of a rounded character-shape, since inscribing straight lines would have split the grain of the leaf.

Each Indian script is a potent and cherished symbol of its regional language and culture. Traditionally, scribes would use their regional script to write Sanskrit as well as their regional language: many Sanskrit manuscripts produced in medieval Bengal, for example, are in the Bengali character. In modern times, partly as a result of the standardising effect of the print medium, the pan-Indian script of Devanagari has come to be seen as the Sanskrit script *par excellence.* For the Hindi-speaker, therefore, Devanagari is not only the script of everyday modern life, but also the timeless record of an ancient and prestigious culture.

Fig 2: New Delhi roadsigns are written in the capital's four major languages: Hindi, English, Panjabi (Gurmukhi script) and Urdu

Devanagari distinguishes each sound occurring in the Sanskrit language; and it has no characters that are phonetically redundant. The language was elaborately analysed and codified by the grammarians of ancient India, probably in a deliberate attempt to protect this vehicle of sacred utterance from the changes which make their mark on every language over time. This codification, which culminated in the grammatical aphorisms of Pāṇini in about the 4th century BC, went beyond mere grammar into the very *sounds* of the language: it supplied a phonetically systematic syllabary in which each sound was classified according to both the *manner* and *place* of its articulation in the mouth. This beautifully scientific legacy, which you can inspect in the matrix on page 15, is still the basis of the script as used for Hindi today. The main consonant series begins with the sounds *ka kha ga gha*, produced at the back of the throat, and moves gradually forward through such categories as the palatal ('roof of the mouth') sounds *ca cha ja jha* and the dental sounds *ta tha da dha*, to conclude with *ma*, produced by the lips. Thus the syllabary does not follow an arbitrary order like the Roman alphabet, but has a logical sequence determined by phonetics.

Although the grammar and orthography of Sanskrit were fixed for all time by the grammarians, the natural process of linguistic change continued over the centuries, gradually producing a range of derivative languages and dialects whose generic names portray their perceived relationship to the so-called 'polished' or 'refined' language of Sanskrit: Prakrit was the ancient 'common' or 'natural' speech, and its early medieval successor Apabhramsha the 'corrupt' speech. These languages themselves gave birth to the regional Indo-Aryan languages of today, such as Hindi, Bengali, Panjabi, Sinhala – in fact, most of the languages of the subcontinent except the Dravidian foursome of Tamil, Telugu, Kannada and Malayalam, which constitute a language family in their own right. The three historical periods of language development (or rather 'decline', to follow the Indian conception of a progressive falling away from the perfection of Sanskrit!) are now labelled Old, Middle and New Indo-Aryan – or OIA, MIA, and NIA. NIA languages such as Hindi mostly developed within the last 1000 years, and have substantial literary traditions starting in about the 14th century AD. As is the case with the relationship between modern European languages and their ancient forbears Greek and Latin, the NIA languages are grammatically much simpler than the OIA languages.

Modern Hindi is based on the Hindi dialect called Khaṛī Bolī, whose homeland is the Delhi area. Hindi could be described as the granddaughter of Sanskrit (even if the family line has been cross-fertilised from other stock over the years); and that well-loved grandparent is still very much present in the family home, supplying a large number of loanwords and neologisms from her great jewel-box of vocabulary. But despite this close domestic harmony, there is something of a generation gap in matters of writing. Hindi has been influenced by languages and cultures which were unknown to India in the first millennium AD when Devanagari came into being, and so the Devanagari script, tailor-made for the phonology of Sanskrit, sits slightly less perfectly on the phonology of the younger language. As a result, Devanagari has had to be altered a little here and there in order to fit the new requirements. These modifications mostly deal with sounds which came to India as part of the legacy of Perso-Arabic culture that played such an important part in the life of North India from the 11th century AD onwards.

Hindi and Urdu

It is the use of the Devanagari script that most clearly distinguishes Hindi from its sister-language, Urdu. The two languages share the same grammar and a very large stock of vocabulary and idiom; and at the level of everyday colloquial conversation they are effectively one and the same. Let us look at an example. The sentence 'Your son does not work very hard' could be expressed as *āpkā laṛkā bahut mehnat nahī̃ kartā* (literally, 'Your boy much labour not does'). This is perfectly natural everyday Hindi; it is also perfectly natural everyday Urdu. But when written, the two languages *look* entirely different:

Hindi	आपका लड़का बहुत मेहनत नहीं करता ।
Urdu	آپکا لڑکا بہت محنت نہیں کرتا ۔

The Hindi version is written in the Devanagari script; the Urdu version is written in the Perso-Arabic script, which runs from right to left. (As used for Urdu, the Perso-Arabic script has some small modifications to allow it to show Indo-Aryan features like the retroflex *ṛ*, which do not occur in Persian or Arabic.) Take writing out of the picture, and you have a language which could be called 'Hindi-Urdu', and which could claim to be the world's third largest language in terms of numbers of speakers. But of course writing is actually very much *in* the picture, and so we have not a single language (and literature), but two complementary ones; and not many people are familiar with both the Devanagari *and* the Urdu writing systems. The political and cultural history of South Asia has forced an increasing distance between Hindi and Urdu. Hindi finds the roots of its cultural heritage in Sanskrit, and augments the Hindi-Urdu vocabulary stock by borrowing words from Sanskrit or by constructing them on a Sanskrit base; Urdu has a similar relationship with Persian and Arabic. This has meant that Hindi has acquired a Hindu cultural resonance, while Urdu resonates with Islamic culture; and when India was partitioned in 1947, Hindi became the official language of India (alongside English), while Urdu, still widely used in India by Muslims and Hindus alike, became the national language of the newly created nation of Pakistan.

Fig 3: A clinic sign in Hindi, English and Urdu. Sadly, use of the Urdu script is declining in India.

The example of the 'lazy boy' given above does, of course, over-simplify a complex issue; and a few more things need to be said before we leave the bittersweet relationship between Hindi and Urdu. Firstly, the fact that Hindi and Urdu have different cultural orientations means that they have developed quite separately over the last century and a half. The moment one leaves the context of lazy boys and begins to discuss issues that call for a higher register of vocabulary (concepts for which English draws on

Latinate vocabulary, such as education, economics, religion and so on), the divide between Hindi and Urdu becomes very clear indeed, and whether written or spoken, the one language may well cease to be intelligible to a speaker of the other. Despite their common ancestry, it is no longer accurate to describe Hindi and Urdu as 'one language with two scripts', for neither language can function fully without the higher vocabularies that they draw from Sanskrit and Perso-Arabic respectively.

Secondly, even within our example sentence it is possible to force a divide between Hindi and Urdu styles. Let us see how the sentence is made up. The pronoun *āpkā* 'your', the noun *laṛkā* 'boy', the adjective *bahut* 'much' and the negated verb *nahī̃ kartā* 'not does' are part of the shared Hindi-Urdu stock – they belong to the dialect of Khaṛī Bolī, which is the basis of Hindi-Urdu; and their ancestry can ultimately be traced back to Sanskrit. The noun *mehnat,* 'labour', very common in Hindi-Urdu, is a loanword from Persian (and has an Arabic ancestry). A 'purist' who wanted to lend the sentence a more Sanskritic tone might substitute the Sanskrit loanword *pariśram* for *mehnat* and might also substitute the Sanskrit loanwords *putră* and *adhik* for the Sanskrit-derived (but not actually Sanskrit) *laṛkā* and *bahut* respectively. The sentence would then have the characteristics of *śuddh* or 'pure' Hindi, and its resulting formal flavour might be translated as 'Your son is not exceedingly industrious'. Some people like this kind of language; they feel that it shows education, sophistication and high culture, and they relish its specifically Sanskritic, and hence Hindu, stamp; others might well feel it to be artificial and contrived. Speakers of 'pure' Urdu have a harder task in attaining linguistic 'purity', because although they may succeed in giving the sentence a nicely Persian flavour by incorporating Perso-Arabic synonyms for some words, the pronouns and the verb system belong historically to the family of languages descended from Sanskrit; but a similar process of substitution, replacing Hindi-Urdu words with Perso-Arabic ones, can make an Urdu sentence hard for a Hindi-speaker to understand.

The common ground of Hindi and Urdu, as exemplified by our 'lazy boy' sentence, is often called 'Hindustani', meaning '[the speech] of Hindustan, northern India'.

Fig 4: In this banner for Girish Karnad's play तुग़लक, 'Tuglak', *the title is styled to suggest the Islamic character of its subject, a 14th-century Turkish ruler of India*

How Devanagari works: a 'garland of syllables'

This book takes a practical approach to teaching the script, and does not discuss the detail of phonetic analysis; works listed in the bibliography address these matters. (Phonetic terminology used in this book is explained in an appendix.) But it is important to grasp a few basic principles about how the script works, so please don't skip the following paragraphs!

The script runs from left to right. There is no concept of a distinction between upper and lower case; neither is there a particular cursive style – handwriting follows the printed forms more or less closely in most respects, although of course it cuts some corners, and style varies quite a lot from writer to writer. Some examples of Hindi handwriting are given in Appendix 1.

The basic unit of Devanagari is the *syllable,* called *akṣar* or *varṇă*, rather than the individual letter as is the case in the Roman script; so Devanagari is strictly speaking not an 'alphabet' but a 'syllabary' (the Indian term *varṇă-mālā*, 'garland of syllables', puts it more poetically). Each basic consonant contains within it a following *'a'* vowel, pronounced like the 'a' in 'alert'; thus the character क represents not just the consonant *k* but the syllable *ka*, and the character स represents *sa* – in both cases a consonant with its free bonus, the so-called 'inherent' vowel *a*.

The other vowels are marked with signs (called *mātrā*) attached to the consonant. For example:

क + ा	gives	का	*kā*
क + ु	gives	कु	*ku*
क + े	gives	के	*ke*

Similarly, सु is *su* and से is *se*.

A vowel that *doesn't* follow a consonant, however, is written differently: it has a full, independent character of its own. So while the word *ke* is written के, the word *ek* (which *begins* with the vowel) is written एक – in which *e* is ए. This difference between vowel *signs* and vowel *characters* will be explained fully later on. Individual characters are referred to by the suffix *-kār* (literally '-maker'), as in *kakār* for क ('the character *ka*'), *sakār* for स, *ākār* for आ.

Conjunct characters

When a consonant is followed by another consonant with no vowel coming between them, a 'conjunct' consonant is born, as in क्स *ksa*, in which क *ka* and स *sa* have coalesced into a single syllable, and the '*a*' vowel normally inherent in क *ka* has been suppressed. This process takes a little getting used to, and we'll be spending quite some time on it later.

Purity of vowels

In articulating Hindi vowels, particularly *e* and *o*, it is essential to maintain a pure pronunciation – one in which the quality of the vowel *does not change* during the period of its articulation. Such vowels are quite different from the diphthongs of English: the vowel in the word 'say' (as pronounced in southern England) is actually a sequence in which one sound shades off into another – as you will hear if you pronounce the word slowly and deliberately. A similar process applies with the English word 'go'. By contrast, the Hindi sounds *e* and *o* (like the French words 'est' and 'eau' respectively) have a steady, unchanging quality that can be held in pronunciation indefinitely, or at least until the breath runs out.

A similar 'purity' must be attempted in the production of other vowels in Hindi. In English, vowels are much affected by their adjacent sounds: the long vowel in the word 'keel' becomes a diphthong 'kee-yul' because of the following 'l' (compare 'keel' with 'keep', where the vowel is unchanged) and is therefore different from the pure *ī* in the Hindi word *kīl*, meaning 'nail'. Similarly, in American and some other varieties of English, a vowel is coloured by a following 'r' (say 'world' in an American accent, comparing 'BBC World News' with 'CNN World News'), and this too has to be avoided in Hindi.

Aspirated and unaspirated consonants

Two other contrasts in Hindi are very important. The first is a contrast between *aspirated* and *unaspirated* consonants. 'Aspiration' is the breath which is released from the mouth as a sound is produced; there is always *some* aspiration – 'unaspirated consonant' is an exaggeration if not a misnomer! – but the varying amount determines the sound produced. In English, the amount of aspiration depends largely on context. The consonant 'p' usually has a fairly strong aspiration: say the word 'pin' loudly with your hand in front of your mouth, and you will feel the puff of air. By contrast, 'bin' will produce much less puff; but so, interestingly, will 'spin' – showing that the breathiness of 'p' is reduced after the sound 's', even if that contrast isn't recognised in the spelling of the English word.

Hindi has distinctive pairs of unaspirated and aspirated consonants, the first of which is usually *less* aspirated than the English equivalent, the second *more* aspirated. Practise saying *pan* (the first syllable of the word

'Panjāb'; it rhymes with 'fun' and 'bun', not 'fan' and 'ran') until you have reduced the aspiration of the 'p' to the level encountered in the English word 'bun'; this will give you the unaspirated consonant. Then, to produce the aspirated sound *pha* (as in *phal*, 'fruit'), practise *increasing* the aspiration of *ph*. Indian scripts have fully independent characters for unaspirated and aspirated consonants respectively – they don't simply add an 'h' as we have to do in Roman transliteration; Hindi-speakers hear them as different sounds, even if English-speakers often don't. Here are some examples:

प	*pa*
फ	*pha*
ब	*ba*
भ	*bha*

Retroflex and dental consonants

The second contrast is that between 'retroflex' and 'dental' consonants. The English sounds 't', 'd', 'n' etc. are produced by the tongue touching the 'alveolar ridge' – that part of the palate between the upper teeth and the place where the roof of the mouth opens into a large cavern. Indo-Aryan languages, however, have two contrasted sets of such consonants: the retroflex and the dental. Retroflex consonants are produced by curling the tip of the tongue back to strike the roof of the mouth at the rear part of the alveolar ridge. This produces a consonant sound which is 'harder' than English consonants. (Retroflex sounds are transliterated with dots under the Roman letter: *ṭ*, *ḍ*, etc.) Most Indian speakers of English use these retroflex sounds for the English 't' and 'd', making the sounds characteristically harder than they are in standard English; this is part of the characteristic sound of Indian English. By contrast, the Hindi 'dental' consonants are produced with the relaxed tip of the tongue touching the back of the upper teeth, producing a much 'softer' sound than in English, and more akin to consonants such as the 't' in French 'temps' or Italian 'tempo'. The dentals are transliterated without dots.

The following diagrams show the position of the tongue for retroflex consonants (on the left) and dental consonants (on the right):

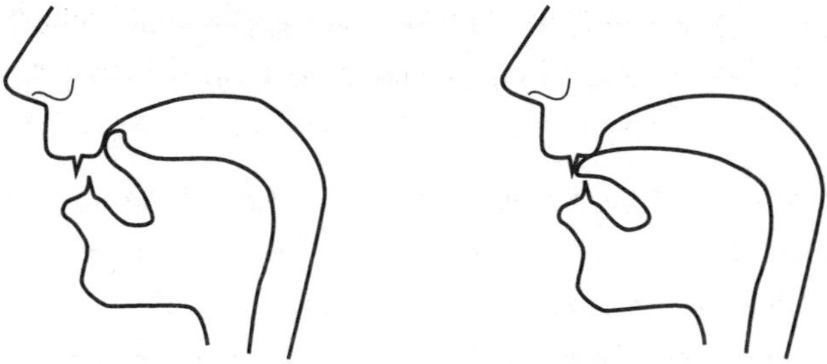

What you see and what you get

Generally, the phonetic basis of Devanagari script gives a close connection between writing and speech – it's very much a user-friendly, 'what-you-see-is-what-you-get' writing system. But there are a few exceptions to this:

A. The 'inherent vowel' *a* is usually unpronounced at the end of a word (except in words of one syllable like *na* 'not'): thus the name spelt *rāma* is pronounced 'Rāma' in Sanskrit but usually 'Rām' in Hindi. If a word ends in two consonants, however, the inherent vowel often has to be lightly pronounced in order to articulate both consonants clearly: an example is the last syllable in the word *mitră* 'friend', pronounced with a light final '*a*', which is transcribed as '*ă*' in this book.

B. Whereas Sanskrit distinguished between the palatal *ś* (pronounced like 'sh' in English 'ship') and the cerebral or retroflex *ṣ* (pronounced with the tongue curled back), Hindi has all but lost the phonetic distinction between the two; most speakers pronounce both as 'sh', allowing *āśā*, 'hope' to rhyme with *bhāṣā*, 'language' – unless the *ṣ* appears in the same syllable as another retroflex consonant, as in *spaṣṭ,* 'clear, evident'. Thus the distinction between the two exists as a historical spelling only, rather as is the case with 'ph' and 'f' in English (compare 'sophisticated' with 'sofa').

c. Similarly, *ṛ*, which had the status of a vowel in ancient India, is now pronounced as identical to *ri* by most speakers (although sometimes as *ra* or *ru,* particularly in western India). Hence the short 'i' sound in *kṛpā,* 'kindness'.

On page 15 is a matrix showing the basic elements of Devanagari. The matrix is for reference – you don't have to learn it all at once, as its elements will be introduced gradually in the pages that follow. It follows the classical order established for Sanskrit in ancient times, in which the characters were arranged according to how and where they were produced in the mouth. This order – with vowels preceding consonants – is also used as the dictionary order.

2 UNIT 2
The Devanagari syllabary

Independent vowel characters

अ a	आ ā	इ i	ई ī
उ u	ऊ ū	ऋ ṛ	
ए e	ऐ ai	ओ o	औ au

Consonants

क	ka	ख	kha	ग	ga	घ	gha	(ङ्	ṅ)*
च	ca	छ	cha	ज	ja	झ	jha	(ञ्	ñ)*
ट	ṭa	ठ	ṭha	ड	ḍa	ढ	ḍha	ण	ṇa
त	ta	थ	tha	द	da	ध	dha	न	na
प	pa	फ	pha	ब	ba	भ	bha	म	ma

य ya	र ra	ल la	व va
श śa	ष ṣa	स sa	ह ha

Dependent vowel signs (combined with क् k)

क ka	का kā	कि ki	की kī
कु ku	कू kū	कृ kṛ	
के ke	कै kai	को ko	कौ kau

*These forms do not occur independently, and can be ignored for now.

Here is the main part of the matrix again, showing the phonetic organisation of the sounds. Notice how this main block of consonants (from क *ka* to म *ma*) is organised according to two criteria: vertically, showing the nature or quality of the sound; and horizontally, showing the place of articulation in the mouth.

	UNVOICED		VOICED		
	unasp.	aspirated	unasp.	aspirated	nasal
velar	क ka	ख kha	ग ga	घ gha	ङ ṅ
palatal	च ca	छ cha	ज ja	झ jha	ञ ñ
retroflex	ट ṭa	ठ ṭha	ड ḍa	ढ ḍha	ण ṇa
dental	त ta	थ tha	द da	ध dha	न na
labial	प pa	फ pha	ब ba	भ bha	म ma

Dotted characters

Seven of the Devanagari consonants also appear in 'dotted' forms (such as क़ and ज़), not shown in the classical matrix; dotted characters are used for sounds that did not exist in Indian languages when Devanagari was first developed. Here are the seven dotted forms.

क़ *qa* ख़ *<u>kh</u>a* ग़ *<u>g</u>a* ज़ *za* ड़ *ṛa* ढ़ *ṛha* फ़ *fa.*

Whenever Hindi acquired a new sound that didn't exist in Sanskrit, and which was therefore not catered for in the Devanagari script, it modified whichever character came closest to it; for example a Persian 'q' sounded closest to 'k' and was therefore written with a modified form of क. Some such sounds developed earlier, during the Middle Indo-Aryan stage, and others were imported into India in languages such as Persian and English.

The 'flap' sound *ṛa* and its aspirated equivalent *ṛha* came into being during the MIA period. To write it, a subscript dot was added to the signs for *ḍa* and *ḍha* respectively:

ड़ *ṛa* based on ड *ḍa*

ढ़ *ṛha* based on ढ *ḍha*

Take care not to confuse two similar transliteration characters here: *ṛa* stands for ड़, while *r̥* (with a small subscript circle rather than a dot) stands for ऋ. Most books that refer to Indian languages use *ṛ* for both, and because of the relative rarity of ऋ *r̥* in Hindi, this causes no confusion in practice.

In the medieval period, Hindi began to absorb vocabulary from the languages of cultures that came to India from outside. Persian and Arabic, and subsequently Portuguese and English, were particularly rich sources of loanwords, and Hindi cannot now function without them (the name 'Hindi' is itself a Persian word!). These languages included sounds which again were unknown – and therefore had no script sign – in indigenous Indian languages. The remaining five 'dotted' characters were developed to indicate the pronunciation of these new sounds. Again, the character nearest in pronunciation to the new sound was adapted by adding a subscript dot:

क़ *qa*	based on क *ka*
ख़ *<u>kh</u>a*	based on ख *kha*
ग़ *g̱a*	based on ग *ga*
ज़ *za*	based on ज *ja*
फ़ *fa*	based on फ *pha*

These sounds are all included in the description of the sounds of Hindi that follows in Unit 3. It is important to recognise the difference between the dotted and undotted characters, because the dot may distinguish between two otherwise identical words: thus खाना *khānā* means 'food', while ख़ाना *<u>kh</u>ānā* means 'compartment' or 'place of work' (as in डाक-ख़ाना *ḍāk-khānā* 'post office').

Although it is important to be aware of such differences as you learn the script, many speakers do not regularly distinguish dotted characters from their undotted equivalents, both saying and writing क *ka* for क़ *qa* (e.g. कलम *kalam* for क़लम *qalam,* 'pen'), ज *ja* for ज़ *za* (e.g. रजाई *rajāī* for

Fig. 5: Dotted characters are often written without their dots, as in this poster for Sanjay Gupta's film ख़ौफ़ khauf *('Fear')*

रज़ाई *razāī,* 'quilt'), फ *pha* for फ़ *fa* (e.g. फेल *phel* for फ़ेल *fel,* 'fail'), and so on. While some speakers don't distinguish dotted characters either in writing or in speech, others will omit the dots when writing, but will pronounce the sound as though it *were* dotted; in short, the writing conventions are in a state of transition, and there is little consistency. For the learner, it's best to maintain the difference between dotted and undotted characters as a matter of course.

This short unit has shown you the basic character set for Devanagari. It is now time for us to move on and look at the individual characters themselves. Remember that the phonetic basis of Devanagari makes it best to learn each character in conjunction with its pronounced sound; so while you practise writing the characters you should also note the instructions about their pronunciation.

UNIT 3
Consonants

This unit shows you how to write and pronounce the consonant and semi-vowel characters. You should practise copying the handwritten forms, several times each, speaking them aloud as you do so. Here are some important watchpoints:

- Write on *lined* paper.
- Use a relatively fine pen; a fountain pen is ideal because it gives the best control.
- Copy the handwritten examples, not the printed forms.
- Make sure that the characters are well-proportioned, and don't write them larger than the handwritten examples.
- Each character should 'hang' from the upper line and occupy about two-thirds of the space between the lines – don't be tempted to sit the characters on the line below in the manner of the Roman script.
- Each character is drawn from left to right, starting at the lower left side and concluding with the horizontal top line; follow the sequence shown in the examples.
- Ensure that the characteristic shape of the character is clearly and boldly written; characters should not slant or become straggly.

Your practice format should look something like this:

क क क क

ख ख ख ख

ग ग ग ग

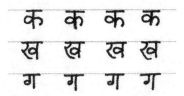

As you begin practising Devanagari you will find that it is rather more like writing in Roman block capitals than writing in the cursive style of English handwriting. Remember that there is no concept of distinctive 'upper and lower cases' in Indian scripts.

When writing a whole word, finish each character by adding its top line before moving on to the next; only when you feel completely at home in the script and need to write faster should you take the short-cut of writing all the top line across a whole word in a single stroke.

Some characters have a small break in the top line (ध *dha*, भ *bha*); this must be carefully maintained, to prevent the characters becoming confused with similar ones without such a break (घ *gha*, म *ma*).

Some English words or phrases are used here to help describe the Hindi sounds. Say them emphatically *out loud*, pronouncing every consonant of the English words, to get the right effect.

Velar consonants

Produced by the back of the tongue touching the 'velum' (soft palate).

क क 

ka as 'k' in 'skin'; aspiration minimal

क़ क़

qa a 'k' sound, but further back in the throat; many speakers substitute क *ka*

ख ख 

kha aspirated version of क ka; as 'k...h' in 'look here!', strongly aspirated. (The closed base of the *printed* character distinguishes ख *kha* from रव *rava*; it is not usually followed in handwriting.)

ख़ 

k̲h̲a as 'ch' in Scottish 'loch' or in German 'Bach'; some speakers substitute ख *kha.*

ग 

ga as 'g' in 'again'

ग़ 

g̲a a guttural 'g' sound found in Perso-Arabic loanwords only; many speakers substitute ग *ga*

घ 

gha aspirated version of ग *ga*; as 'g-h' in 'dog-house' or in 'big hat', spoken fast

ङ 

ṅa the nasal like the 'n' in 'uncle'; it does not occur on its own, but only in certain conjuncts (see Unit 6). You won't need to write it – just note its existence and move on.

Palatal consonants

Produced by the middle of the tongue touching the hard palate.

च 

ca as 'ch' in 'eschew'.

छ 

cha aspirated version of च *ca*; as 'ch...h' in 'touch him!', but with more aspiration

ज 

ja as 'j' in 'jade', or the 'dj' in 'adjacent'

ज़ 

za as 'z' in 'zoo'; some speakers substitute ज *ja*

झ 

jha aspirated version of ज *ja*; as 'dge...h' in 'dodge him!', but with much more aspiration [alternate form झ]

ञ 

ña the nasal like the 'n' in 'unjust'; it does not occur on its own, but only in conjuncts (see Unit 6); it does not occur on its own, and you won't need to write it – just note its existence and move on

Retroflex consonants

Produced by the tip of the tongue curling back to touch the roof of the mouth; see the diagram on page 13. The sound is 'harder' than in English consonants and has no real equivalents.

ट 

ṭa as 't' in 'train', but retroflex

ठ 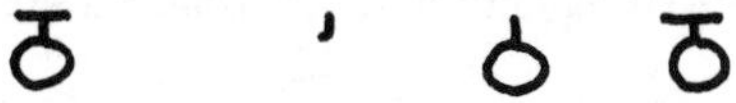

ṭha strongly aspirated version of ट; a bit like 't-h' in 'ant-hill'

ड 

ḍa as 'd' in 'date', but retroflex

ड़ ड़

ṛa as ड *ḍa*, but pronounced as a fast 'flap' – the curled-back tongue briefly flaps past the palate at the ड *ḍa* position

ढ 

ḍha strongly aspirated version of ड *ḍa*

ढ़ ढ़

ṛha strongly aspirated version of ड़ *ṛa*

ण 

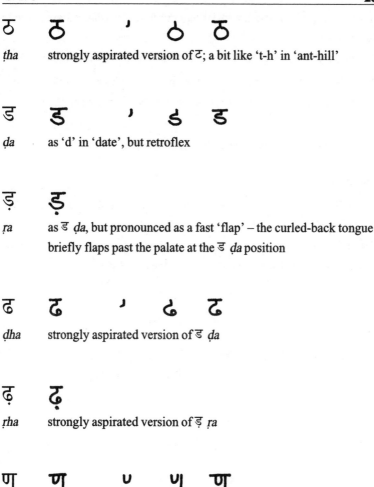

ṇa as 'n' in 'end', but retroflex; some speakers substitute न *na*. [alternate form ण]

Doing the exercises

Now that we're more than halfway through the consonants, it's time to begin some more reading and writing practice. Although these exercises are primarily concerned with the form and sound of the words, each word is followed by its English translation; and fuller translations are given in the glossary.

- When doing any of the exercises, *always read the words aloud.*
- When you are asked to 'transcribe', you should *read, copy and transcribe* all Devanagari words into the Roman script, and vice versa.
- You will find a key to the exercises in Appendix 4.

Exercise 1

Remembering that the inherent vowel is silent at the end of a word, transcribe the words below. (An asterisk in this first exercise marks the translation of Hindi words that are specialised or uncommon; and words with exclamation marks are commands – see unit 5.)

खग	चख	जग	खट	झट
bird*	eye*	world	knocking	instantly
कच	गज	टक	डच	डग
hair*	elephant*	stare*	Dutch	stride
kaṇ	*ṭhan*	*jaṭ*	*ṭhaṭh*	*kaṭ*
particle	clanging	Jat	crowd*	cut!
gaṇ	*jaj*	*ḍhak*	*ghaṭ*	*ṭhag*
group	judge	cover!	pitcher	bandit

Dental consonants

Produced by the tip of the tongue touching the edge of the teeth at the point where the teeth emerge from the gum; see the diagram on page 13. The sound is 'softer' than in English consonants – more like in French or Italian, or in Scots dialect.

त 

ta touch the top of the tip of your tongue to the back of your upper front teeth (!) and try to say 'tell'

थ 

tha Position the tongue as for त above and, without letting the tongue protrude through the teeth, say 'think!' emphatically

द 

da Position the tongue as above and say 'then!'

ध 

dha strongly aspirated version of द *da;* as above but breathe out

न 

na as 'n' in 'anthem'

Labial consonants

Produced by the lips.

प 

pa as 'p' in 'spin'; aspiration minimal

फ 

pha strongly spirated version of प *pa*; as 'p-h' in 'top-hat'

फ़ फ़

fa as 'f' in 'fin'

ब ब 

ba as 'b' in 'bin'

भ भ 

bha strongly aspirated version of ब *ba*; as 'b-h' in 'club-house', spoken quickly

म म 

ma as 'm' in 'man'

Exercise 2

Transcribe the following words:

तन	गज़	धन	फट	पद
body	yard	wealth	at once	position
मत	तब	मन	जब	गत
opinion	then	mind	when	last, past

And into Devanagari:

paṛh	*maṭh*	*<u>kh</u>at*	*ḍaph*	*pab*
read!	monastery	letter	a drum	pub
nag	*bam*	*kap*	*path*	*paṭ*
gem	bomb	cup	path	board

Semi-vowels etc.

The first and last are semi-vowels; the middle two are alveolars.

य 

ya as ‘y’ in ‘yes’, but less tightly pronounced. In final position, in words like भय *bhay* and समय *samay,* it is pronounced to rhyme with ‘may’ (but without the diphthong).

र 

ra as ‘r’ in ‘serene’; unlike English ‘r’ in ‘far’, it is always pronounced. It does *not* colour the preceding vowel as in the American pronunciation of ‘firm’.

ल 

la as the *first* ‘l’ in ‘label’, but more dental. It does *not* colour the preceding vowel as in the English pronunciation of ‘keel’.

व 

va between a ‘v’ and a ‘w’: has less tooth–lip contact than in ‘vine’, but the lips are less rounded than in ‘wine’. A final -ā*v* is pronounced as *-āo*: thus the name राव *rāv* is pronounced *rāo* (and spelt ‘Rao’ in English).

Sibilants

श 

śa as ‘sh’ in ‘shell’

ष 

ṣa although technically retroflex, this is not regularly distinguished from *śa* except in combination with retroflexes such as *ṭa* or *ṭha*; occurs in Sanskrit loanwords only

स 

sa as 's' in 'sell'

Aspirate

ह 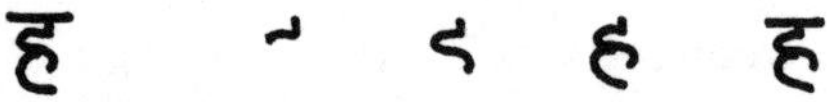

ha as 'h' in 'ahead' – a fully voiced sound. In medial position it lightens an adjacent '*a*' vowel; thus both vowels in महल *mahal* sound like the 'e' in 'mend'. In final position after *a*, it can be replaced by an *ā* sound: बारह *bārah* pronounced '*bārā*', जगह *jagah* pronounced '*jagā*'.

Congratulations: you have now met *all* the consonants. It's time to extend our range into three-consonant words:

कमल	*kamal*	lotus
गरम	*garam*	warm, hot
नगर	*nagar*	town
बरस	*baras*	year
नमक	*namak*	salt
तरह	*tarah*	way, manner
नहर	*nahar*	canal

Exercise 3

Celebrate your mastery of the consonants by doing this further transcription exercise! Transcribe the following words:

दल	दस	कम	हम	घर	हल	मन
party	ten	less	we	home	plough	mind
तरफ़	बचत	सड़क	नरम	ख़बर	महल	नगर
direction	saving	road	soft	news	palace	town

And into Devanagari:

had	*pal*	*vaṭ*	*sac*	*nal*	*har*	*sab*
limit	moment	banyan	true	tap	each	all
jaṛ	*ḍar*	*bhay*	*bas*	*śak*	*haq*	*tay*
root	fear	fear	control	doubt	right	decided
jagah	*bhajan*	*gazal*	*samay*	*magar*	*lagan*	*qalam*
place	hymn	ghazal	time	but	devotion	pen

UNIT 4
Vowels

Vowel characters

These are independent forms used at the *beginning* of a syllable, as explained on page 10.

अ अ 

a as 'a' in 'alert' [alternate form ऄ]

आ आ

ā as 'a' in 'father'

इ इ 

i as 'i' in 'in'

ई ई 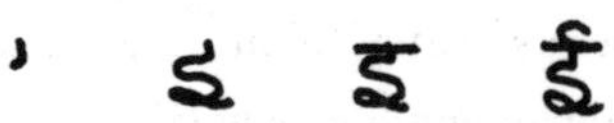

ī as 'ee' in 'feet'

उ उ 

u as 'u' in 'put'

ऊ 

ū as ‘oo’ in ‘spoon’

ऋ 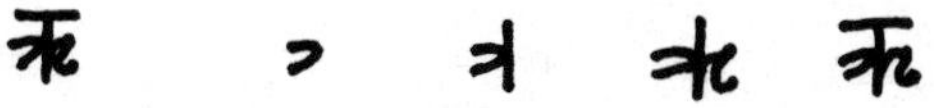

ṛ as ‘ri’ in ‘riddle’ (though in some western areas it is pronounced as ‘ru’ in ‘ruin’ or as the ‘ru’ in ‘rut’); the sound was classified as a vowel in Sanskrit, and it occurs in Sanskrit loanwords only

ए 

e similar to the ‘e’ in ‘tent’, but longer, closer to the French ‘é’; *not* a diphthong – it does *not* rhyme with ‘may’

ऐ 

ai similar to the ‘a’ in ‘bank’ but with the mouth less open; in eastern parts of the Hindi-speaking area it becomes more diphthongised, rhyming with ‘my’

ओ 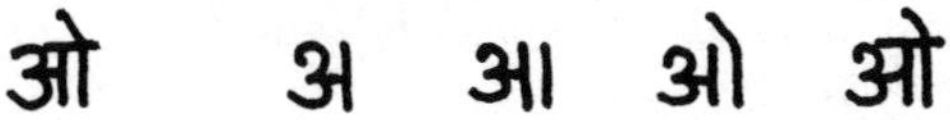

o similar to the first part of ‘o’ in ‘hotel’, but closer to the French ‘eau’; *not* a diphthong – does *not* rhyme with ‘go’

औ 

au as ‘o’ in ‘office’ (in eastern parts of the Hindi-speaking area it becomes more diphthongised, more like ‘ow’ in ‘cow’)

Let us now look at these vowels within whole words:

अ	अमर	*amar*	immortal
आ	आम	*ām*	mango
इ	इधर	*idhar*	here
ई	ईख	*īkh*	sugarcane
उ	उमर	*umar*	age
ऊ	ऊब	*ūb*	boredom
ऋ	ऋण	*ṛṇ*	debt
ए	एक	*ek*	one
ऐ	ऐश	*aiś*	luxury
ओ	ओर	*or*	direction
औ	और	*aur*	and

The word और *aur* 'and' also has the meaning 'more, other, different'. In these meanings it is pronounced with a heavy stress (एक और *ek aur* 'one more'), whereas it has very *little* stress when meaning 'and'.

Exercise 4

Transcribe the following words, each of which begins with a vowel character:

ऐ	असर	ओस	ऋण	आह
hey!	effect	dew	debt	sigh
आग	अगर	आदर	औरत	ऊन
fire	if	respect	woman	wool

And into Devanagari:

ūpar	*umas*	*ā*	*o*	*āj*
up	sultriness	come!	oh	today
ekaṛ	*īd*	*aṭal*	*aur*	*alag*
acre	Eid	immovable	and	separate

Vowel signs

When a vowel immediately follows a consonant, it is not written with the independent characters just introduced, but with a sign, the *mātrā,* attached to the consonant. *This sign replaces the inherent vowel.* Compare the following:

ऊन	*ūn*	wool
ख़ून	*<u>kh</u>ūn*	blood

While ऊन *ūn* is written with the independent *ū* character ऊ (because the vowel comes at the beginning of the syllable), ख़ून *<u>kh</u>ūn* is written with the sign ू following the consonant ख़, whose inherent 'a' vowel it replaces.

Unlike a vowel character, a vowel sign is 'dependent' on the consonant: it cannot be used alone.

The following section shows the forms and usage of the 10 vowel signs from आ *ā* to औ *au.* The pronunciation of these vowels has already been explained in the section on vowel characters. Reading the examples will also help you become more familiar with the consonants; you should copy each Hindi word out several times, saying it aloud as you do so.

1. आ *ā* Written with the sign ा after the consonant, as in का *kā*:

काम	*kām*	work
दाल	*dāl*	lentils

नाम	*nām*	name
सात	*sāt*	seven
साथ	*sāth*	with
हाथ	*hāth*	hand
कान	*kān*	ear
नाक	*nāk*	nose

Here are some words with two long *ā* vowels:

दादा	*dādā*	grandfather
बाज़ार	*bāzār*	market
ताला	*tālā*	lock
राजा	*rājā*	king
सारा	*sārā*	whole, entire
खाना	*khānā*	food
सामान	*sāmān*	luggage

Exercise 5

Transcribe the following menu items, which contain a mixture of long and short (*a*/*ā*) vowels:

गाजर	सलाद	चावल	चना	पालक
carrot	salad	rice	chickpea	spinach

And into Devanagari:

masālā	*śarāb*	*parāṭhā*	*kabāb*	*maṭar*
spice	alcohol	paratha	kebab	pea

2. इ *i* Written with the sign ि *before* the consonant that it follows in pronunciation, as in कि *ki*, this vowel sign is quite exceptional – all the others are written after, above or below the consonant.

फिर	*phir*	then
रवि	*ravi*	Ravi
पिता	*pitā*	father
लिपि	*lipi*	script
शिकायत	*śikāyat*	complaint
किताब	*kitāb*	book
सिख	*sikh*	Sikh
सितार	*sitār*	sitar

The word सितार *sitār* is of Persian origin and means 'three-string', and derives from a time when the instrument was much less developed than the multi-stringed sitar of classical Indian music. The word तार *tār* is the everyday word for 'wire' in Hindi – and by extension also means 'telegram' (just as 'wire' used to in English in the days when telegrams were in common use). A 'wireless' is usually called रेडियो *reḍiyo* in Hindi; the more colourful synonym, बेतार *betār* ('without wire') is, sadly, seldom heard.

3. ई *ī* Written with the sign ी after the consonant, as in की *kī*:

भी	*bhī*	also
मीनार	*mīnār*	tower
पानी	*pānī*	water

चीनी	*cīnī*	sugar
सीता	*sītā*	Sita
बीस	*bīs*	twenty
नीला	*nīlā*	blue
सीटी	*sīṭī*	whistle

Exercise 6

Transcribe the following words:

मीटर	बिना	पीतल	हिसाब	दिल	ठीक
metre	without	brass	account	heart	OK

And into Devanagari:

nāmī	*qīmat*	*kahānī*	*sāṛī*	*sikh*	*śikāyat*
famous	price	story	sari	Sikh	complaint

4. उ *u* Written with the sign ु beneath the consonant, as in कु *ku*:

कुछ	*kuch*	some
कुमार	*kumār*	Kumar
सुख	*sukh*	happiness
तुम	*tum*	you
बहुत	*bahut*	very; much
पुलिस	*pulis*	police
कुल	*kul*	total

Where do these roads lead? (See foot of page.)

5. ऊ *ū* Written with the sign ू beneath the consonant, as in कू *kū*:

भूख	*bhūkh*	hunger
सूखा	*sūkhā*	dry
फूल	*phūl*	flower
धूप	*dhūp*	sunshine
दूध	*dūdh*	milk
दूर	*dūr*	far
झूठ	*jhūṭh*	lie
भूमि	*bhūmi*	earth

There's an exception here: the consonant र carries its *u* and *ū* vowels to the *right* of the character– रु *ru,* रू *rū* – and *not* below. Notice how the long रू *rū* has a curl that is absent in short रु *ru.*

रूप	*rūp*	form, beauty
रुपया	*rupayā*	rupee

[Answer: Varanasi; Allahabad – spelt *ilāhābād* in Hindi]

गुरु	*guru*	guru
शुरू	*śurū*	beginning

Exercise 7

Transcribe the following words:

पुल	धूल	रूखा	सूद	दूरी	कबूतर
bridge	dust	harsh	interest	distance	pigeon

And into Devanagari:

sūkhā	*ruko*	*tū*	*rūs*	*tum*	*mulāyam*
dry	stop!	you	Russia	you	soft

6. ऋ *ṛ* Written with the sign ृ beneath the consonant, as in कृ *kṛ*.

कृपा	*kṛpā*	kindness
मृग	*mṛg*	deer
तृण	*tṛṇ*	blade of grass
हृदय	*hṛday*	heart

Note the special way in which ऋ combines with ह as हृ, in this last word.

7. ए *e* Written with the sign े above the consonant, as in के *ke*.

मेला	*melā*	fair (festival)
देश	*deś*	country
केवल	*keval*	only
मेज़	*mez*	table

सेवा	*sevā*	service
रेखा	*rekhā*	line
सेब	*seb*	apple
केला	*kelā*	banana

Where do these roads lead? (See foot of page.)

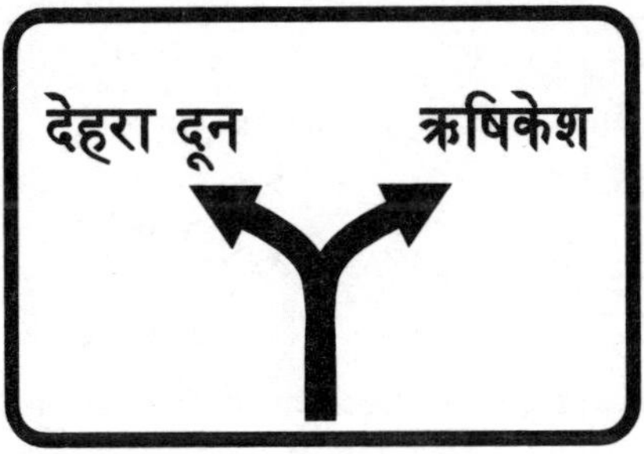

8. ऐ *ai* Written with the sign ै above the consonant, as in कै *kai*:

मैला	*mailā*	dirty
है	*hai*	is
थैला	*thailā*	bag
बैठा	*baiṭhā*	seated, sitting
शैली	*śailī*	style
चुड़ैल	*cuṛail*	witch
भैया	*bhaiyā*	brother
पैदा	*paidā*	born, produced

[Answer: Dehra Dun; Rishikesh]

Exercise 8

Transcribe the following words:

केवल	खेती	पैसे	बेटा	मेज़	ख़ैरियत
only	farming	money	son	table	well-being

And into Devanagari:

bekār	*pahelī*	*mailā*	*sinemā*	*terā*	*ṭhekedār*
useless	riddle	dirty	cinema	your	contractor

9. ओ *o* Written with the sign ो after the consonant, as in को *ko.*

मोर	*mor*	peacock
शोर	*śor*	noise, racket
पड़ोसी	*paṛosī*	neighbour
लोग	*log*	people
सो	*so*	so
रेडियो	*reḍiyo*	radio
कोका-कोला	*kokā-kolā*	Coca-Cola

Where do these roads lead? (See foot of page.)

[Answer: Jaisalmer; Devikot]

10. औ *au* Written with the sign ौ after the consonant, as in कौ *kau*.

नौ	*nau*	nine
सौ	*sau*	hundred
पौधा	*paudhā*	plant
के दौरान	*ke daurān*	during
नौकर	*naukar*	servant
दौलत	*daulat*	wealth
हौले	*haule*	softly
मौत	*maut*	death

Hindi has many words for 'death', including मौत *maut* (from Arabic) and मृत्यु *mṛtyu* (from Sanskrit) – and, in spoken Hindi, the English loanword डेथ *ḍeth* (which takes its feminine gender from the other two).

Fig 6: A शौकर *śaukar is a 'shocker' – a shock-absorber!*

Exercise 9

Transcribe the following words:

धोखा	कोमल	हौज़	दौड़ो	कोठी
trick	soft	tank	run!	mansion

And into Devanagari:

bolo	*jau*	*gorā*	*maulik*	*karoṛ*
speak!	barley	fair (pale)	original	crore

It's very important to understand the difference between the dependent vowels (vowel *signs*) and independent vowels (vowel *characters*). Turn back to the explanation on page 33, and then read the paired examples given below:

				FIRST VOWEL IS:
a	मगर	*magar*	but	inherent
	अगर	*agar*	if	independent
ā	भाषा	*bhāṣā*	language	dependent
	आशा	*āśā*	hope	independent
i	सिर	*sir*	head	dependent
	इधर	*idhar*	over here	independent
ī	धीरे	*dhīre*	slowly	dependent
	ईमान	*īmān*	honesty	independent
u	पुल	*pul*	bridge	dependent
	उधर	*udhar*	over there	independent
ū	लूट	*lūṭ*	loot	dependent
	ऊन	*ūn*	wool	independent

ṛ	कृषि	*kṛṣi*	agriculture	dependent
	ऋषि	*ṛṣi*	sage	independent
e	पेट	*peṭ*	stomach	dependent
	एकाध	*ekādh*	one or two	independent
ai	पैसा	*paisā*	money	dependent
	ऐनक	*ainak*	spectacles	independent
o	सो	*so*	so	dependent
	ओस	*os*	dew	independent
au	मौसी	*mausī*	aunt	dependent
	औरत	*aurat*	woman	independent

It's not only at the *beginning* of words that the independent forms are used. They are also used *within* a word, as the second of two vowels in sequence: for example, the *ī* vowel in बाईस *bāīs,* 'twenty-two', must be written in its independent form (because it follows another vowel, not a consonant).

बाईस	*bāīs*	twenty-two
तेईस	*teīs*	twenty-three
कई	*kaī*	several
भाई	*bhāī*	brother
ताऊ	*tāū*	uncle
सूअर	*sūar*	pig
चाहिए	*cāhie*	needed
बुआ	*buā*	aunt

Relationship terms are much more specific in Hindi than they are in English: मौसी *mausī* 'mother's sister'; मौसा *mausā* 'husband of mother's sister'; नानी *nānī* 'mother's mother'; दादी *dādī* 'father's mother'; चाचा *cācā* 'father's younger brother'; ताऊ *tāū* 'father's elder brother'; बुआ *buā* 'father's younger sister' and so on.

Finally, here are some words consisting of vowel characters only:

आई	*āī*	(she) came
आए	*āe*	(they, masc.) came
आओ	*āo*	come!
आइए	*āie*	please come!

Exercise 10

Transcribe the following words, remembering that vowels not following a consonant must be written with the vowel *character*, not the vowel sign:

gae went $^{\text{m.pl}}$	gaī went^{f}	gāī sang^{f}	gāo sing!	jāega will go
dhoo wash!	*dhoie* wash!	*dhoe* washed$^{\text{m.pl}}$	*ruī* cotton	*raīs* aristocrat
rulāī crying	*soī* slept^{f}	*banāe* made$^{\text{m.pl}}$	*banāo* make!	*baṛhaī* carpenter

Nasalised vowels and *candrabindu*

Any Hindi vowel (except the Sanskrit ऋ *ṛ*) can be nasalised – the vowel is pronounced with a nasal quality, as if you had a cold in the nose. In writing, nasality is shown by the sign ँ which, logically enough, is called *candrabindu*, 'moon [and] dot'; *anunāsik*, 'nasalisation', is an alternative name. It sits above the middle of the character, and in our transliteration system it is marked by a tilde (˜) above the vowel. Some other systems use a dotted 'm' (*ṃ* or *ṁ*) following the vowel: thus आँ = *ā̃* = *āṃ* = *āṁ*.

हँसी	*hãsī*	laughter
हाँ	*hā̃*	yes
इँचीटेप	*ĩcīṭep*	tape-measure
कुआँ	*kuā̃*	well
कुएँ	*kuẽ*	wells
बहुएँ	*bahuẽ*	daughters-in-law
हूँ	*hū̃*	am
ऊँचा	*ū̃cā*	high

When a syllable has a vowel sign above the top line, there's no room for the 'moon', so the dot alone is used. It sits just to the right of the vowel sign. With a long ई *ī*, it sits *within* the little loop above the line, as in the second of the following examples:

सिंघाड़ा	*sĩghāṛā*	water chestnut
गईं	*gaī̃*	went (f.pl)
नहीं	*nahī̃*	no, not
में	*mẽ*	in
मैं	*maĩ*	I
हैं	*haĩ*	are

घरों में	*gharõ mẽ*	in the houses
होंठ	*hõṭh*	lip
चौंतीस	*caũtīs*	thirty-four

You'll have noticed that the transliteration remains the same whether the moon is visible or eclipsed by a vowel sign.

Many writers and typesetters dispense with the moon altogether, and use the dot alone all the time, giving हां etc. Inconsistency rules!

Whereas English has *pre*positions (which precede the noun, as in 'in the houses') Hindi has *post*positions (which follow the noun, as in घरों में *gharõ mẽ* 'in houses'). Before a postposition, a noun changes from the 'direct' case to the 'oblique' case; in this example, direct plural घर *ghar* has changed to oblique plural घर *gharõ*. Other postpositions are पर *par* 'on', से se 'from, with', तक tak 'up to, until'.

Exercise 11

Transcribe the following words:

गाँव	महँगा	आँगन	पूँछ	धुआँ	अँधेरा
village	expensive	courtyard	tail	smoke	darkness

And into Devanagari:

khā̃sī	*saũph*	*donõ*	*laũg*	*ā̃ī̃*	*mezẽ*
cough	fennel	both	clove	came$^{f.pl}$	tables

5 UNIT 5
Simple sentences and commands

This book cannot take you very far into the grammar of Hindi, but you will find it useful to know how some basic sentences are formed.

Requests and commands are formed very simply. But these 'imperative' verbs also demonstrate an important characteristic of Hindi – its elaborate 'honorific' system which allows you to address someone in either an intimate, familiar or formal style. Each level has its own pronoun for the word 'you':

INTIMATE (for small children etc.)	तू	*tū*
FAMILIAR (for friends etc.)	तुम	*tum*
FORMAL (for all others)	आप	*āp*

Each pronoun has its own imperative verb form; but before we come to that, we must look at the *infinitive* form of the verb. The infinitive consists of two parts – a 'stem' (the base for several verb forms), and the ending *-nā*. Here are some common verbs in the infinitive:

बोलना	*bolnā*	to speak
पूछना	*pūchnā*	to ask
बुलाना	*bulānā*	to call

The imperatives are formed as follows:

तू	*tū*	stem alone	बोल	*bol*
			पूछ	*pūch*
			बुला	*bulā*

तुम	*tum*	stem + *o*	बोलो	*bolo*
			पूछो	*pūcho*
			बुलाओ	*bulāo*
आप	*āp*	stem + *-ie*	बोलिए	*bolie*
			पूछिए	*pūchie*
			बुलाइए	*bulāie*

These आप *āp* imperative endings, and some other similar verb endings, can also be written with a य् *y* between the two vowels: बोलिये *boliye,* पूछिये *pūchiye,* बुलाइये *bulāiye.*

Legend has it that in the days of the Raj the British memsahibs, indifferent to real Hindi, would learn simple Hindi commands by assimilating them to English phrases: 'There was a banker' was to be interpreted by servants as representing दरवाज़ा बंद कर *darvāzā band kar,* 'Close the door', and 'There was a cold day' meant दरवाज़ा खोल दे *darvāzā khol de,* 'Open the door'. Thankfully, those days are long gone.

Let us now look at some pronouns and the verb 'to be'.

मैं	*maĩ*	I	हूँ	*hũ*	am
यह	*yah*	this, he, she, it	है	*hai*	is
वह	*vah*	that, he, she, it	है	*hai*	is
तुम	*tum*	you (familiar)	हो	*ho*	are
आप	*āp*	you (formal)	हैं	*haĩ*	are
ये	*ye*	these, they	हैं	*haĩ*	are
वे	*ve*	those, they	हैं	*haĩ*	are

यह *yah* (often pronounced '*ye*') is used to refer to a nearby person or thing, like 'this' in English; वह *vah* (usually pronounced '*vo*')is used for a remote person or thing, like 'that' in English. The plural forms are ये *ye* and वे *ve* respectively (though in speech, *vo* is as common as *ve*).

The subject of the sentence comes at the beginning, and the verb at the end. You can form many sentences with nouns, pronouns and 'to be':

मैं राहुल हूँ ।	*maĩ rāhul hũ.* I am Rahul.
यह आदमी राम है ।	*yah ādmī rām hai.* This man is Ram.
देवनागरी आसान है ।	*devanāgarī āsān hai.* Devanagari is easy.
तुम कौन हो ?	*tum kaun ho?* Who are you?
यह क्या है ?	*yah kyā hai?* What is this?
वे क्या हैं ?	*ve kyā haĩ?* What are they/those?

You will have figured out the meanings of these words:

आदमी	*ādmī*	man
आसान	*āsān*	easy
कौन	*kaun*	who
क्या	*kyā*	what

(This last word, क्या *kyā*, combines क and य in a single character: these 'conjuncts' are introduced in the next unit.)

Interrogative words ('question words') in Hindi mostly begin with क्, just as they mostly begin with 'wh' in English: कब *kab* 'when', कहाँ *kahā̃* 'where', कौन *kaun* 'who', क्या *kyā* 'what', क्यों *kyõ* 'why' and so on.

The word क्या *kyā* can also be used to transform a statement into a question: the sentence यह आसान है *yah āsān hai* means 'this is easy', while क्या यह आसान है ? *kyā yah āsān hai?* means 'is this easy?'.

क्या यह आदमी राम है ?	*kyā yah ādmī rām hai?* Is this man Ram?
क्या देवनागरी आसान है ?	*kyā devanāgarī āsān hai?* Is Devanagari easy?

These basic sentence patterns will make it easy for you to practise writing and speaking simple sentences, and to *use* the words that you are learning to read and write.

Some more information about nouns, adjectives and gender is given in Unit 8.

UNIT 6
Conjunct consonants

This unit shows you how to read and write 'conjunct' characters. Just when you thought you'd learnt all the consonant characters, here are some new variations! But most conjuncts are quite straightforward.

What is a conjunct? When two consonants are pronounced with no vowel between them, the two consonants are usually physically joined together to form a single unit – two characters 'conjoined' as one.

Let's take a common English loanword to see how it works. The phonetic basis of the word 'school' in Hindi is *skūl* – its pronunciation being very close to the English (although the *l* is dental, softer-sounding than in English). The Devanagari components needed to form this word are as follows:

स	क	ू	ल
sa	*ka*	*ū*	*l*

We have already seen how the '*ū*' vowel replaces the inherent '*a*' vowel in क *ka*. This gives us:

स	कू	ल
sa	*kū*	*l*

But we also need to kill off the inherent vowel in स *sa*, otherwise the word will read *sakūl*. That inherent vowel can theoretically be removed by adding a little sign called *virām* or *halant* just below the character:

स *sa* becomes स् *s*

But *virām* isn't much used in real writing; it's mostly restricted to technical contexts such as this explanation of the script that you're reading now. Instead, the inherent '*a*' vowel is removed by forming a 'conjunct' character, in which two characters are physically joined to each other. This is a much more elegant solution.

Thus स is reduced to स् and then joined to क, forming स्क. To complete the *skū* syllable we just add *ū* – स्कू, giving स्कूल *skūl*.

Does this mean there's a whole new set of characters that has to be learned? Well, yes and no – but mostly no. Most conjuncts are formed quite simply by dropping the *right-hand component of the first member* and attaching it physically to the *entire second member*.

It's (almost) as simple as that, and all that's left to do is to familiarise yourself with the individual ways in which the two component characters join each other to form the conjunct. The simple principle of 'drop the right-hand component of the first member' holds good for most characters built on a vertical line (क, ख, ग, म, ल, श, स etc.), even if the individual shapes of the characters means that the dropped portion will vary a little from character to character. First of all, let's stay with स as the first member and put it through its paces with varying second members.

(In the matter of conjuncts, the semi-vowels य, र, ल and व are not distinguished from consonants. And among these, र is again a special case that will be dealt with separately later.)

स्	+	ट	=	स्ट	स्टेशन	*sṭeśan*	station
स्	+	त	=	स्त	नमस्ते	*namaste*	greeting
स्	+	थ	=	स्थ	स्थान	*sthān*	place
स्	+	म	=	स्म	स्मृति	*smṛti*	memory
स्	+	य	=	स्य	स्याही	*syāhī*	ink
स्	+	व	=	स्व	स्वर	*svar*	note, tone

Exercise 12

Transcribe the following words, which contain conjunct characters (Roman letters that make up a Devanagari conjunct are here shown in **bold** type):

स्थिति	स्वरूप	स्थायी	पिस्तौल	लस्टम-पस्टम
situation	shape	permanent	pistol	somehow or other

And into Devanagari:

sv*āgat*	*ba****st****ī*	***sl****eṭ*	*rā****st****ā*	***sn****ān*	***sm****araṇ*
welcome	slum	slate	road	bathing	recollection

Other characters based on a vertical line will achieve their conjunct form in a very similar way – by simply dropping that vertical line. The list below gives examples of such characters as first members of a conjunct, with a varying set of second members.

ख्	+	य	=	ख्य	ख्याति	*khyāti*	fame
ग्	+	य	=	ग्य	ग्यारह	*gyārah*	eleven
च्	+	छ	=	च्छ	अच्छा	*acchā*	good
ज्	+	व	=	ज्व	ज्वाला	*jvālā*	blaze
ण्	+	ड	=	ण्ड	अण्डा	*aṇḍā*	egg
त्	+	म	=	त्म	आत्मा	*ātmā*	soul
ध्	+	य	=	ध्य	ध्यान	*dhyān*	attention
न्	+	द	=	न्द	हिन्दी	*hindī*	Hindi
प्	+	त	=	प्त	सप्ताह	*saptāh*	week
ब्	+	ज़	=	ब्ज़	सब्ज़ी	*sabzī*	vegetable
भ्	+	य	=	भ्य	सभ्य	*sabhyă*	civilised
म्	+	भ	=	म्भ	आरम्भ	*ārambh*	beginning

ल्	+	प	=	ल्प	कल्प	*kalp*	aeon
व्	+	य	=	व्य	व्यस्त	*vyast*	busy
श्	+	क़	=	श्क़	इश्क़	*iśq*	passionate love
स्	+	ट	=	स्ट	स्टेशन	*sṭeśan*	station

सप्ताह *saptāh* is a Sanskrit loanword meaning 'week'. A more colloquial synonym is the Persian loanword हफ़्ता *haftā*. Both words derive from words meaning 'seven' – सप्त *sapta* in Sanskrit (yielding सात *sāt* in Hindi) and हफ़्त *haft* in Persian. These words for 'seven' are in turn related to Latin 'septem' etc.

Some conjuncts consist of the same member repeated – a *doubled* consonant. In pronunciation, a doubled consonant is 'held' slightly, giving each of the two members its full value. (A similar holding of a doubled consonant occurs with the two 't's in the English phrase 'fat tissue', as compared to the single 't' in 'fat issue'.)

च्	+	च	=	च्च	बच्चा	*baccā*	child
म्	+	म	=	म्म	अम्मा	*ammā*	mother
ल्	+	ल	=	ल्ल	दिल्ली	*dillī*	Delhi
स्	+	स	=	स्स	अस्सी	*assī*	eighty

Not all consonants share the basic shape of स, with its convenient right-hand vertical line. In क and फ, part of the character extends to the right *beyond* the vertical line; and as the first member of conjuncts, these characters lose nothing more than the extreme part of that right-hand extension: thus क becomes क् and फ becomes फ् :

क्	+	स	=	क्स	अक्सर	*aksar*	often
फ़्	+	ल	=	फ़्ल	फ़्लू	*flū*	flu

Other characters don't have a vertical line at all. How such characters join the following member will vary according to their respective shapes, and in many cases, it's the *second* member which has to do most of the changing.

ट्	+	ट	=	ट्ट	छुट्टी	*chuṭṭī*	holiday
ट्	+	ठ	=	ट्ठ	चिट्ठी	*ciṭṭhī*	note, chit
ड्	+	य	=	ड्य	ड्योढ़ी	*ḍyoṛhī*	porch
द्	+	ग	=	द्ग	भगवद्गीता	*Bhagavadgītā*	
द्	+	ध	=	द्ध	बुद्ध	*buddha*	Buddha
द्	+	भ	=	द्भ	उद्भव	*udbhav*	origin
ह्	+	ल	=	ह्ल	आह्लाद	*āhlād*	rapture

These examples show how the second member may appear *below* or *within* the first member. In order to fit in such an awkward position, it sometimes has to be modified in form and reduced in size a little: notice the shape that भ has to assume when it hangs below the belly of द in द्भ and how ल is miniaturised to fit within the middle of ह्ल. (This is a good place to remind you of the special shape of the syllable हृ – not actually a conjunct, but *h* followed by *ṛ*.)

> Many speakers ease the pronunciation of an initial conjunct by prefixing a short 'epenthetic' vowel, usually *i*. Thus the Hindi forms of 'school' and 'station' may be pronounced *iskūl, isṭeśan*. This prefixed vowel is not usually written, though इस्टेशन etc. is a possible spelling.

Exercise 13

Transcribe the following words (Roman letters that make up a Devanagari conjunct are here shown in **bold** type):

नक़्शा	ब्राह्मण	पत्थर	कोष्टक	क्यों	निश्चय
map	Brahmin	stone	bracket	why	decision

And into Devanagari:

*bi**ll**ī*	*hi**nd**ū*	*nā**śt**ā*	*tu**mh**ārā*	*a**dhy**āpak*	*ava**śy**ă*
cat	Hindu	breakfast	your(s)	teacher	certainly
*pa**kk**ā*	***zy**ādā*	*qi**sm**at*	*ha**ty**ā*	*na**ṣṭ***	*ha**ld**ī*
firm	more	fate	murder	ruined	turmeric
*fai**kṭ**arī*	*a**ks**ar*	*la**nd**an*	*ā**tm**ā*	*gira**ft**ār*	*sa**ty**ă*
factory	often	London	soul	arrest	truth

Special conjunct forms

There are just a few more points to be made on this rather time-consuming business of conjuncts.

In most of the examples we've seen so far it's been possible to recognise the individual components of a conjunct, even if they're considerably modified in their conjoined forms. But there are a few conjuncts which are not just the sum of their component parts but, rather, a new form that is quite stylised and/or may look quite unlike its two components. These have to be learnt specially. Conjuncts including र *ra* are a special case and will be dealt with later.

क्	+	त	=	क्त	**क्त**
			=	क्त	**क्त**
क्	+	ष	=	क्ष	**क्ष**
त्	+	त	=	त्त	**त्त**
द्	+	द	=	द्द	**द्द**

द्	+	म	=	द्म	द्म
द्	+	य	=	द्य	द्य
द्	+	व	=	द्व	द्व
श्	+	व	=	श्व	श्व
			=	श्व	श्व
ष्	+	ट	=	ष्ट, ष्ट	ष्ट ष्ट
ह्	+	न	=	ह्न	ह्न
ह्	+	म	=	ह्म	ह्म
ह्	+	य	=	ह्य	ह्य
ह्	+	ल	=	ह्ल	ह्ल

Here are some words illustrating these conjuncts:

शक्ति	शक्ति	*śakti*	power
शक्ति	शक्ति	*śakti*	power
अक्षर	अक्षर	*akṣar*	character, syllable
कुत्ता	कुत्ता	*kuttā*	dog
भद्दा	भद्दा	*bhaddā*	clumsy
पद्म	पद्म	*padmă*	lotus

विद्या	विद्या		*vidyā*	knowledge
द्विज	द्विज		*dvij*	Brahmin
श्वेत	श्वेत		*śvet*	white
श्वेत	श्वेत		*śvet*	white
नष्ट, नष्ट	नष्ट	नष्ट	*naṣṭ*	destroyed
अह्मद	अह्मद		*ahmad*	Ahmad
आह्लाद	आह्लाद		*āhlād*	rapture
चिह्न	चिह्न		*cihn*	sign
सह्य	सह्य		*sahyă*	bearable

The word अक्षर *akṣar* means 'a character, syllable'. Its literal meaning 'imperishable, irreducable' reflects the fact that it is the *syllable* (and not the 'letter', as in the Roman script) that forms the basic building block of the Devanagari writing system.

Fig 7: 'Be aware' of special conjuncts like त्त tta also!

Conjuncts with र *ra*

As we have already seen when looking at the forms रु *ru* and रू *rū,* the character र *ra* is the joker in Devanagari's pack. In conjuncts it has two different forms, depending on whether it is the first or the second member.

When र is the *first* member of a conjunct it is written as a little hook, as in र्म *rma*, above the second member. Be very clear about the sequence here – this र is pronounced *before* the other member of the conjunct:

र्	+	ज़	=	र्ज़	फ़र्ज़	*farz*	duty
र्	+	त	=	र्त	कर्तव्य	*kartavyă*	duty
र्	+	म	=	र्म	धर्म	*dharm*	religion
र्	+	व	=	र्व	पार्वती	*pārvatī*	Parvati

This flying form of र is called *reph*. When the second member of the conjunct bears one of the vowel signs ा, ि, ी, े, ै, ो, ौ the *reph* is written at the extreme *right* of the resulting syllable:

र्	+	मा	=	र्मा	शर्मा	*śarmā*	Sharma (surname)
र्	+	थि	=	र्थि	आर्थिक	*ārthik*	financial
र्	+	थी	=	र्थी	विद्यार्थी	*vidyārthī*	student
र्	+	मों	=	र्मों	धर्मों में	*dharmõ mẽ*	in religions
र्	+	मे	=	र्मे	धर्मेतर	*dharmetar*	secular

When र is the *second* member of a conjunct it is written as a little angled line tucked into the lower part of the first member, as म्र *mra*, as far to the left as possible. Be clear about the sequence here too: this र is pronounced *after* the other member of the conjunct.

ग्	+	र	=	ग्र	ग्राम	*grām*	gram
द्	+	र	=	द्र	दरिद्र	*daridră*	poor
प्	+	र	=	प्र	प्रेम	*prem*	love
ब्	+	र	=	ब्र	ब्राह्मण	*brāhmaṇ*	Brahmin
भ्	+	र	=	भ्र	भ्रष्ट	*bhraṣṭ*	corrupt
ह्	+	र	=	ह्र	ह्रस्व	*hrasvă*	short

In the meaning 'gram' (the unit of weight), the word ग्राम *grām* is of course a loanword from English. But ग्राम is also a Sanskrit word meaning 'village', and is the source of the usual Hindi word for 'village', गाँव *gā̃v*. By a natural process of phonetic erosion, the conjunct ग्र has been reduced over time to ग, and the consonant म has been reduced to the semi-vowel व, with a memory of the nasal quality of म seen in the nasalisation of the long vowel; see page 86 for more on these processes.

Several such conjuncts have special forms:

क्	+	र	=	क्र	क्रिकेट	*kriket̩*	cricket
ट्	+	र	=	ट्र	ट्रक	*t̩rak*	truck
ड्	+	र	=	ड्र	ड्राइवर	*d̩rāivar*	driver
त्	+	र	=	त्र	मित्र	*mitră*	friend
श्	+	र	=	श्र	श्री	*śrī*	Mr

Are you certain about the all-important difference of sequence explained above? Here are some contrasted pairs:

कर्म	*karm*	action
क्रम	*kram*	sequence
शर्म	*śarm*	shame
श्रम	*śram*	toil
गार्ड	*gārd̩*	guard
ग्राम	*grām*	village; gram

The word कार्यक्रम *kāryăkram* 'programme' contains two र conjuncts – the first conjunct (र्य) has र as the *first* component, and the second (क्र) has र as the *second* component. कार्यक्रम is a Sanskrit compound of कार्य *kāryă* 'action, work', and क्रम *kram* 'sequence, order'.

Fig 8: Shri Cement Limited has a brilliant logo that can be read in at least two ways – as श्री śrī *in Hindi, as 'SCL' in English, and perhaps as 'sri' in English too!*

The conjunct ज्ञ *jña*

The conjunct ज्ञ *jña* appears in some Sanskrit loanwords, mostly related to the Sanskrit verb root *jñ-*, 'to know'; the Sanskrit root is cognate with English 'know' and with Greek 'gnosis' etc. In Hindi, this conjunct is usually pronounced *gy*: thus *jñān* is pronounced *gyān*.

ज् + ञ = ज्ञ

ज्ञान	*jñān* (pr. 'gyān')	knowledge
अज्ञेय	*ajñey* (pr. 'agyey')	unknowable
विशेषज्ञ	*viśeṣajñă* (pr. 'viśeṣagyă')	specialist
कृतज्ञ	*kṛtajñă* (pr. 'kṛtagyă')	grateful
अविज्ञ	*avijñă* (pr. 'avigyă')	ignorant
आज्ञा	*ājñā* (pr. 'āgyā')	command

Conjuncts of three or more consonants

Occasionally you may come across conjuncts having more than two components; many of these are in Sanskrit words, although English loanwords too often call for quite complex conjunct-clusters. They follow exactly the same principles as already explained, with 'medial' members behaving like 'first' members:

क् + ट् + र	=	क्ट्र	ऐक्ट्रेस	*aikṭres*	actress
म् + प् + य	=	म्प्य	कम्प्यूटर	*kampyūṭar*	computer
क् + स् + प् + र	=	क्स्प्र	एक्स्प्रेस	*ekspres*	express
त् + स् + य	=	ट	ज्योत्स्ना	*jyotsnā*	moonlight
न् + द् + र	=	न्द्र	इन्द्र	*indră*	Indra
ष् + ट् + र	=	ष्ट्र	राष्ट्र	*rāṣṭră*	nation
स् + त् + र	=	स्त्र	स्त्री	*strī*	woman

Fig 9: पुरुष puruṣ *means 'man' and* स्त्री strī *means 'woman': learn these words at your convenience!*

Using *virām* instead of a conjunct

When conjuncts get too complex, the sign *virām* (see p. 51) can come to the rescue. For example, because hanging a *u* vowel under the already complex conjunct द्भ *dbha* is a tall order, (giving द्भु as in अद्भुत *adbhut*, 'wondrous'), the simpler *virām*-based form द्‌भु (giving अद्‌भुत) is often preferred. Similarly, the font used for printing this book cannot 'stack' a repeated ड one above the other to form a double-decker conjunct as one might in handwriting (ड्ड), and must be content with a ड्‌ड, as in अड्‌डा *aḍḍā* 'stand (for buses etc.)'.

Fig 10: This tailor's signboard uses virām *in the three-member conjunct 'nṭs' in* जेन्ट्‌स jenṭs, *'Gents'*

Exercise 14

The following words have been written using *virām*, as if using a type-writer. Rewrite them using proper conjuncts:

छुट्‌टी	बुद्‌ध	मुहल्‌ला	बच्‌चा	अट्‌ठाईस	गद्‌दा
holiday	Buddha	district	child	eighteen	mattress

चित्त	विद्यार्थी	द्वीप	सह्य	पद्म	चिह्न
mind	student	island	bearable	lotus	sign

Conjuncts using *anusvār*

This section is about a short cut that simplifies the writing of conjuncts involving a nasal consonant, of which there are five. If you look back to the matrix on page 15, you will see that each of the five horizontally arranged consonant categories includes its own nasal consonant. Theoretically, a consonant cannot form a conjunct with any nasal other than the one in its own category: thus dental द can only conjoin dental न (as in हिन्दी, 'Hindi'), and retroflex ड can only conjoin retroflex ण (as in भण्डार, 'store'). The principle behind this restriction is that when the tongue is positioned for one sound, such as a dental, it cannot by definition pronounce any other, such as a retroflex. Here's the full set of five nasal consonants, with examples; remember that the first two nasal consonants, ङ् *ṅ* and ञ् *ñ*, occur in conjuncts *only* – they never stand alone.

ङ्	+	ग	=	ङ्ग	अङ्ग	*aṅg*	limb
ञ्	+	ज	=	ञ्ज	अञ्जन	*añjan*	lampblack
ण्	+	ड	=	ण्ड	अण्डा	*aṇḍā*	egg
न्	+	द	=	न्द	अन्दर	*andar*	inside
म्	+	ब	=	म्ब	कम्बल	*kambal*	blanket

The short cut to achieve the same result is to use a superscript dot called *anusvār* as an alternative to the nasal consonant in the conjunct. Anusvār automatically assumes the same phonetic value as the consonant that follows it: for example, before a dental consonant it stands for the dental न् (half न), and before a retroflex it stands for the retroflex ण् (half ण), and so on. Two different ways of transliterating anusvār are shown below: the first is to maintain the specific nasal consonants used in the examples above, the second is to substitute 'ṃ'. The former system gives a better quide to pronunciation and has been used throughout this book.

अंग	*aṅg/aṃg*	limb
अंजन	*añjan/aṃjan*	lampblack
अंडा	*aṇḍā/aṃḍā*	egg
अंदर	*andar/aṃdar*	inside
कंबल	*kambal/kaṃbal*	blanket

These forms with anusvār are simpler to write than the full conjuncts, and so are usually preferred; in fact, you'll hardly ever see words written with ङ्‍ and ञ these days.

The name 'Hindi' can be written हिन्दी or हिंदी. The word itself means 'the language of Hind', 'Hind' being the Persian name for North India. 'Hind' derives from the name of the river सिंधु 'Sindhu'. Thus the Persian-derived words 'Hindi' and 'Hindu' describe the cultures 'beyond' the Sindhu'; and this river name is known in English as 'Indus', from which the word 'India' derives.

Anusvār is not normally used in doubled consonants ('geminates'): thus *ann, ammā* are written with full conjunct forms, as अन्न (अन्न), अम्मा.

One or two Sanskrit words used in Hindi end in anusvār. The only common example is एवं *evaṃ* (a formal word for 'and'), which is sometimes written as एवम् and is pronounced *evam.*

Before र *ra,* ल *la* and स *sa,* anusvār approximates to a dental *n* (संस्कृत usually pronounced *sanskṛt*). Before व *va,* it is pronounced as *m* (संवत *samvat*). Before ह *ha,* it is pronounced as a velar *ṅ* (सिंह pronounced *siṅh,* approximating to *siṅg*).

Here's a note to shock the purists: although 'mixed' conjuncts such as न्ड (combining a dental with a retroflex) are theoretically impossible, they are much beloved by signwriters and the like, and are seen very commonly in the real world.

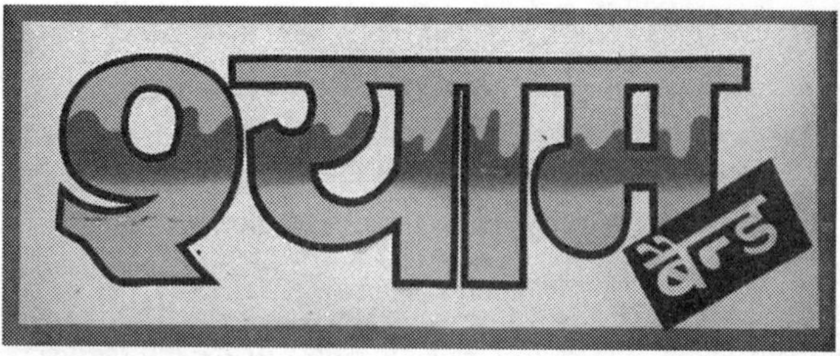

Fig 11: श्याम बैन्ड śyām baiṇḍ *'Shyam Band': the spelling for this wedding band marries a dental* न *to a retroflex* ड *– a banned combination!*

How does anusvār differ from candrabindu/anunāsik? Anusvār stands for a real nasal *consonant*, so that in pronouncing words like हिंदी, कंबल one is actually uttering the full value of 'n' and 'm' respectively. Anunāsik, on the other hand, represents a nasalised *vowel*, so that a word such as हाँ ends without any 'n' or 'm' consonant but has a nasal tone in the vowel itself. Actually, the difference between the two often becomes quite minor in practice – especially when candrabindu drops its moon and becomes identical in form to anusvār!

Exercise 15

Rewrite, replacing anusvār with nasal consonants:

हिंदी	मुंबई	ठंडा	अंग	मनोरंजन
Hindi	Mumbai	cold	limb	entertainment

Rewrite, replacing nasal consonants with anusvār:

मण्डल	भञ्जन	लम्बा	हिन्दू	सङ्घ
circle	breaking	tall	hindu	association
बन्दर	लङ्का	रङ्ग	चिन्ता	घण्टा
monkey	Lanka	colour	anxiety	bell

Fig 12: जैन खादी भन्डार *and* अग्रवाल खादी भंडार *– two adjacent shops* (bhaṇḍār) *selling homespun cotton goods* (khādī). *The first spelling incorrectly conjoins* न *to* ड; *the second uses anusvār, an alternative to the full conjunct form* ण्ड (भण्डार).

When the inherent vowel remains silent

We've already seen that the inherent vowel *a* is not usually pronounced at the end of a word. But sometimes the inherent vowel also remains silent *within* a word. It is difficult to make a watertight rule here, but the following three formulae will account for most instances.

The inherent vowel usually remains silent in the following circumstances:

1. At the end of a word (except monosyllables such as न *na* 'not'). As we saw earlier, the main exception is that the inherent vowel is pronounced (lightly, as 'ă') after any conjuncts that are difficult to pronounce without a following vowel: मित्र *mitră*, कृष्ण *kṛṣṇă.*

2. In the second character of a word whose third character includes a vowel sign. Thus in the word दूसरा *dūsrā,* 'second, other', in which रा *rā* is written with the vowel sign ा *ā*, the inherent vowel of स *sa* is silent.

लड़की	*laṛkī*	(not '*laṛakī*')	girl
चमड़ी	*camṛī*	(not '*camaṛī*')	skin
तरकीब	*tarkīb*	(not '*tarakīb*')	means, plan
सरकार	*sarkār*	(not '*sarakār*')	government
राजधानी	*rājdhānī*	(not '*rājadhānī*')	capital

Exception – When the second or third character is a conjunct:

अस्पताल	*aspatāl*	(not '*asptāl*')	hospital
नमस्ते	*namaste*	(not '*namste*')	greeting
समस्या	*samasyā*	(not '*samsyā*')	problem

3. In the second character of a word of four or more characters.

मसलन	*maslan*	(not '*masalan*')	for example
अफ़सर	*afsar*	(not '*afasar*')	officer
जानवर	*jānvar*	(not '*jānavar*')	animal
लखनऊ	*lakhnaū*	(not '*lakhanaū*')	Lucknow
कलकत्ता	*kalkattā*	(not '*kalakattā*')	Calcutta

In some people's pronunciation, a few words *do* retain a medial inherent vowel when one would expect them to drop it; most such exceptions must be learned individually. The inherent vowel is very short (or 'light').

विकसित	*vikăsit*	developed
के बावजूद	*ke bāvăjūd*	in spite of
जनता	*janătā*	people, the public

Words including a prefix may be 'weighed' as two separate words. Thus लाजवाब *lājavāb*, 'peerless', is pronounced according to its construction as

ला-जवाब, 'without-answer', not as 'लाज-वाब'; and नापसंद *nāpasand,* 'unliked', is pronounced as ना-पसंद, 'not- liked', not as 'नाप-संद'.

A small number of words borrowed from beyond the Indo-Aryan family of languages (and hence not having an established Devanagari spelling) may be written with or without a conjunct:

कुरसी / कुर्सी	*kursī*	chair
परदा/ पर्दा	*pardā*	curtain, purdah
उमदा / उम्दा	*umdā*	good
गरदन / गर्दन	*gardan*	neck

The word जन्म *janmă,* 'birth', is often pronounced *janam*, despite the conjunct; similarly उम्र *umră* is often pronounced *umar* (and is sometimes written उमर *umar*).

Why not use a conjunct *wherever* the inherent vowel is silent? Because, although normally silent, the vowel is still theoretically present; and in contexts such as songs and traditional verse, it may be pronounced.

Finally, here's a list of the hundred most commonly occurring conjuncts.

1	क्	+	क	=	क्क	11	क्	+	स	=	क्स
2	क्	+	ख	=	क्ख	12	ख्	+	य	=	ख्य
3	क्	+	त	=	क्त, क्त	13	ग्	+	द	=	ग्द
4	क्	+	य	=	क्य	14	ग्	+	न	=	ग्न
5	क्	+	र	=	क्र	15	ग्	+	र	=	ग्र
6	क्	+	ल	=	क्ल	16	ग्	+	ल	=	ग्ल
7	क्	+	व	=	क्व	17	ग्	+	व	=	ग्व
8	क्	+	श	=	क्श	18	घ्	+	र	=	घ्र
9	क्	+	ष	=	क्ष	19	च्	+	च	=	च्च
10	क्	+ ष् +	म	=	क्ष्म	20	च्	+	छ	=	च्छ

21	ज्	+	ञ	=	ज्ञ	49	ध्	+	व	=	ध्व
22	ज्	+	र	=	ज्र	50	न्	+	त	=	न्त
23	ट्	+	ट	=	ट्ट	51	न्	+	द	=	न्द
24	ट्	+	ठ	=	ट्ठ	52	न्	+	द् + र	=	न्द्र
25	ट्	+	र	=	ट्र	53	न्	+	न	=	न्न, न्न
26	ड्	+	ड	=	ड्ड	54	न्	+	य	=	न्य
27	ड्	+	र	=	ड्र	55	न्	+	ह	=	न्ह
28	ण्	+	ट	=	ण्ट	56	प्	+	त	=	प्त
29	ण्	+	ठ	=	ण्ठ	57	प्	+	न	=	प्न
30	त्	+	क	=	त्क	58	प्	+	प	=	प्प
31	त्	+	त	=	त्त	59	प्	+	य	=	प्य
32	त्	+	त् + व	=	त्त्व	60	प्	+	र	=	प्र
33	त्	+	थ	=	त्थ	61	प्	+	ल	=	प्ल
34	त्	+	न	=	त्न	62	ब्	+	ज	=	ब्ज
35	त्	+	म	=	त्म	63	ब्	+	द	=	ब्द
36	त्	+	य	=	त्य	64	ब्	+	ध	=	ब्ध
37	त्	+	र	=	त्र	65	ब्	+	र	=	ब्र
38	त्	+	व	=	त्व	66	भ्	+	य	=	भ्य
39	त्	+	स	=	त्स	67	भ्	+	र	=	भ्र
40	द्	+	ग	=	द्ग	68	म्	+	न	=	म्न
41	द्	+	द	=	द्द	69	म्	+	र	=	म्र
42	द्	+	ध	=	द्ध	70	र्	+	त	=	र्त
43	द्	+	भ	=	द्भ	71	र्	+	थ	=	र्थ
44	द्	+	म	=	द्म	72	र्	+	म	=	र्म
45	द्	+	य	=	द्य	73	र्	+	फ	=	र्फ
46	द्	+	र	=	द्र	74	र्	+	व	=	र्व
47	द्	+	व	=	द्व	75	र्	+	स	=	र्स
48	ध्	+	य	=	ध्य	76	ल्	+	म	=	ल्म

77	व्	+	र	=	व्र	89	स्	+ त्	+ र	=	स्त्र
78	श्	+	क	=	श्क	90	स्	+	थ	=	स्थ
79	श्	+	च	=	श्च, श्च	91	स्	+	न	=	स्न
80	श्	+	य	=	श्य	92	स्	+	प	=	स्प
81	श्	+	र	=	श्र	93	स्	+	य	=	स्य
82	श्	+	व	=	श्व, श्व	94	स्	+	र	=	स्र
83	ष्	+	ट	=	ष्ट, ष्ट	95	ह्	+	न	=	ह्न
84	ष्	+ ट्	+ र	=	ष्ट्र	96	ह्	+	म	=	ह्म
85	ष्	+	ण	=	ष्ण	97	ह्	+	य	=	ह्य
86	स्	+	क	=	स्क	98	ह्	+	र	=	ह्र
87	स्	+	ट	=	स्ट	99	ह्	+	ल	=	ह्ल
88	स्	+	त	=	स्त	100	ह्	+	व	=	ह्व

Exercise 16

Identify these geographical names:

चंडीगढ़	औरंगाबाद	इंदौर	गंगा
मध्य प्रदेश	बंगाल	राजस्थान	पाकिस्तान
ग्वालियर	श्रीनगर	पंजाब	गंगोत्री

Transcribe the following into Devanagari (Roman letters that make up a Devanagari conjunct are here shown in **bold** type). The last four are *not* place names, as you will discover in the key.

*di**ll**ī*	*yamuno**tr**ī*	*kalka**tt**ā*	*nāth**dv**ārā*
*u**jj**ain*	*hari**dv**ār*	*vṛ**nd**āban*	*du**rg**āpur*
*mu**mb**aī*	*mahārā**ṣṭr**ă*	*bhubane**śv**ar*	*a**mb**ālā*
*u**tt**ar*	*da**kṣ**iṇ*	*pū**rv**ă*	*pa**śc**im*

7 UNIT 7
Some more writing conventions

Numerals

The Devanagari numerals are fighting a losing battle against their 'Arabic' cousins borrowed from English, which have official sanction in Hindi usage; this is ironic considering that the Arabic numerals themselves derive from India. But it is still essential to be able to recognise the Devanagari numerals. The numerals 1, 5, 8 and 9 have alternative forms, shown here in handwriting only:

0	०		०	शून्य	*śūnyă*
1	१	१	१	एक	*ek*
2	२		२	दो	*do*
3	३		३	तीन	*tīn*
4	४		४	चार	*cār*
5	५	५	५	पाँच	*pā̃c*
6	६		६	छह	*chah*
7	७		७	सात	*sāt*
8	८	८	८	आठ	*āṭh*
9	९	९	९	नौ	*nau*
10	१०		१०	दस	*das*

The numeral २ can show that a word is to be repeated, e.g. for emphasis:

बड़ी २ आँखें = बड़ी बड़ी आँखें *baṛī baṛī ā̃khẽ* great big eyes

Many urban addresses in India feature *section* number followed by *house* number in the formula '1/5'. This formula is more likely to be written in Arabic numerals than in Devanagari numerals nowadays, but you still won't find your destination without knowing the spoken Hindi for this usage, which uses the participle बटे *baṭe* from बटना *baṭnā* 'to be divided':

१/५ (or 1/5) = एक बटे पाँच *ek baṭe pā̃c* one over five

The usual Devanagari equivalent to the use of 'a, b, c' in labelling a sequence of items (such as paragraphs) is क, ख, ग, *ka, kha, ga.* To know the 'ABC' or basic principles of a subject is to know its 'क, ख, ग'. This indicates that the Devanagari syllabary is often conceived of as beginning with the main consonant sequence (see p. 16) rather than the vowels.

Punctuation

Most punctuation in modern Hindi has been adopted from Western languages. The only punctuation sign native to Devanagari is the vertical line (।), used as the full stop or period. It is called दंड *daṇḍă,* 'staff', or खड़ी पाई *khaṛī pāī,* 'upright line'. In traditional poetry, it is doubled (॥) at a verse ending. These days, the Roman full stop is often used in print in place of the खड़ी पाई.

The colon is used rather sparingly: this may be because of potential confusion with the Devanagari sign called *visarg* (see p. 76).

Inverted commas (either single or double) are used to indicate speech, but as with most aspects of Hindi punctuation, the conventions for their use are much less standardised than they are in English.

The convention of writing individual words separately comes from Western languages; in traditional Indian manuscripts, words were written continuously without a break.

Use of the little sequence of dots to indicate a statement or question left 'in suspension' shows an interesting dilemma between the differential conventions of Hindi and English writing: it is sometimes written at the level of the top line (following Devanagari logic), but may be followed by a full stop at the *base* of the characters (following Roman logic):

सीता ग़ायब है ···. *sītā gāyab hai....* Sita is missing... .

The hyphen may be used to help elucidate the noun compounds that are s common in Hindi (e.g. बस-सेवा *bas-sevā,* 'bus service'), but practic varies. A hyphen is more likely to be used if it helps to remove an ambiguity: in the compound भू-खंड *bhū-khaṇḍ,* 'region of the earth', th hyphen removes the danger of any visual or mental association with भूख *bhūkh,* 'hunger', whereas in the compound भूकंप *bhūkamp,* 'earthquake' no hyphen is needed (भूक *bhūk* not being a common word).

Signwriters are fond of playing with script conventions, often mixing Devanagari and English within phrases and even within words Examples noticed recently in Uttar Pradesh include:

- A truck's diesel cap labelled 'D जल', playing on the sense of जल as 'water'. (Remember that ज often replaces ज़ in both pronunciation and writing.)
- A sign reading दर्पण टेरूर्स (for दर्पण टेलर्स 'Darpaṇ Tailors') with the ल reversed as रू – literally reflecting the meaning of the word '*darpaṇ*', 'mirror'.
- A ढाबा or roadside cafe named after its proprietor as 'पंडित G' (i.e पंडित जी) – जी being an expression of respect suffixed to names .
- An autorickshaw slogan reading मेरा १३ ७ (मेरा तेरह सात – to be read, rather unphonetically, as मेरा तेरा साथ, 'Your [and] my company' i.e. 'You and me together'.
- A boutique with the mixed name संस**KRITI**, perhaps indicating the composite 'culture' (संस्कृति) of the goods on sale.

Abbreviations

In English, the individual *letter* is the basic script unit, and is therefore the basis of abbreviations. In Hindi, however, the *syllable* is the basic unit, so the abbreviation of a word constitutes *the whole of the first syllable*, complete with any vowel and/or nasal sign. The abbreviation is followed by '०', a small circle (or sometimes by a full stop):

डा०	=	डाक्टर	*ḍākṭar*	Doctor (Dr)
पं०	=	पंडित	*paṇḍit*	Pandit (Pt)
रु०	=	रुपया/रुपये	*rupayā/ye*	rupee/s (Re, Rs)
स्व०	=	स्वर्गीय	*svargīyă*	the late, deceased

There are two conventions to choose between when writing personal initials: the system just described, and a phonetic transliteration of the pronounced values of the initials in English. So someone called त्रिलोचन नाथ शर्मा *trilocan nāth śarmā*, 'Trilochan Nath Sharma', might write his initials plus surname in either of the two following ways:

त्रि० ना० शर्मा	*tri. nā. śarmā*
टी० एन० शर्मा	*ṭī. en. śarmā*

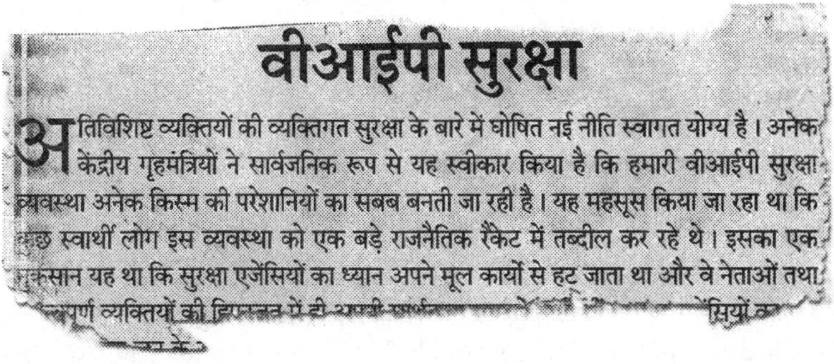

वीआईपी सुरक्षा

अतिविशिष्ट व्यक्तियों की व्यक्तिगत सुरक्षा के बारे में घोषित नई नीति स्वागत योग्य है। अनेक केंद्रीय गृहमंत्रियों ने सार्वजनिक रूप से यह स्वीकार किया है कि हमारी वीआईपी सुरक्षा-व्यवस्था अनेक किस्म की परेशानियों का सबब बनती जा रही है। यह महसूस किया जा रहा था कि कुछ स्वार्थी लोग इस व्यवस्था को एक बड़े राजनैतिक रैकेट में तब्दील कर रहे थे। इसका एक नुकसान यह था कि सुरक्षा एजेंसियों का ध्यान अपने मूल कार्यों से हट जाता था और वे नेताओं तथा [illegible]पूर्ण व्यक्तियों की [illegible]

Fig 13: This newspaper article, which is headed वीआईपी सुरक्षा, vīāīpī surakṣā, *is concerned with security* (सुरक्षा) *for 'VIPs';* वीआईपी *could alternatively have been written* वी० आई० पी०.

With its increasing use of abbreviations for the names of organisations, protocols and the like, India is awash with acronyms these days; and Hindi has taken them up enthusiastically, especially in newspapers. Acronyms are usually written without punctuation, and are pronounced as written:

नभाटा	=	नवभारत टाइम्स	Nav Bharat Times
बसपा	=	बहुजन समाज पार्टी	Bahujan Samaj Party
भाजपा	=	भारतीय जनता पार्टी	Bharatiya Janta Party

Fig 14: What is the registration number of this bus, manufactured by the industrial giant Tata? The first two characters indicate the state in which the bus is registered. (See foot of page.)

Visarg

The sign *visarg* resembles a widely spaced colon and is written without a headstroke, as in दु:ख *duḥkh,* 'sorrow'; as the transliteration with a dotted *ḥ* shows, it is an aspiration equivalent to that of ह् *h* (but unvoiced, and not representing a distinct syllable). In Sanskrit it is pronounced as a lightly breathed echo of the preceding vowel: शान्ति: *śāntiḥ,* 'peace', pronounced as *śāntihi.* It mostly occurs in Sanskrit loanwords and is not very common in Hindi.

[Answer: UP 07/F 8278 (उ.प्र. = उत्तर प्रदेश Uttar Pradesh.]

प्राय:	*prāyaḥ*	generally
छ:	*chaḥ*	six
अत:	*ataḥ*	therefore

Avagrah

The sign *avagrah* has the shape ऽ. It's essentially a Sanskrit sign, having to do with vowel elisions that don't happen in Hindi. In Hindi its main function is to show that a vowel is sustained in a cry or a shout:

आईऽऽऽ! *āīīī!*

In transcribing the words of a song, *avagrah* shows that the preceding vowel is sustained over successive beats:

जाने क्याऽ तू नेऽ कही
jāne kyā-ā tū ne-e kahī
Who knows wha-a-a-t you-ou-ou said

"माँऽऽऽ"

Fig 15: माँ ऽऽऽ – a child's call to its mother.

Rather more technically, avagrah can mark a long syllable in prosody. Here it is contrasted with the vertical line (daṇḍā*)*, which is used to mark short beats. Thus the word चाँदिनी *cā̃dinī*, 'moonlight', would be scanned as ऽ।ऽ, equivalent to ¯˘¯ in Western prosody.

The *praṇav* ॐ, *om*

The sacred syllable '*om*' (or '*aum*'), called the *'praṇav'* ('auspicious sound'), has the special symbol ॐ. It is often written as an invocation or a sign of auspicious well-being, for example at the beginning of a letter or other document, or on doorways, shrines etc.

Writing English words in Devanagari

Hindi uses an ever-growing number of loans from non-Indian languages, mostly English. Many a Hindi-learner, setting off to India with a proudly acquired knowledge of the Hindi script, will find his or her efforts rewarded by encounters with signboards such as the following:

एअर इंडिया *ear iṇḍiyā* Air India

व्हीलर एण्ड कम्पनी प्राइवेट लिमिटेड
vhīlar eṇḍ kampanī prāiveṭ limiṭeḍ
Wheeler & CompanyPrivate Limited

Fig 16: What 'free' facilities are on offer here, and what is the name of the company?

When transliterating English words into Hindi (for example, when writing your name in Devanagari), you should ignore the English spelling and transcribe the phonetic value of the word *as pronounced by a Hindi-speaker.* A Hindi-speaker will hear English 'd' and 't' as closer to the retroflex than to the dental – hence the spelling लिमिटेड, *limiṭeḍ,* above. And Devanagari vowels will also match the pronounced values of the English – hence the spelling एअर, *ear,* in 'Air India'.

The superscript sign ॅ, a dotless moon, is sometimes used above a long आ *ā* (ऑ) for the English vowel in a Hindi-speaker's pronunciation of words such as 'ball', 'law', and the first syllable of 'chocolate'. (Do not confuse it with candrabindu: ऑ is not the same as आँ.) This is a script

[Answer: Registration, road tax, comprehensive insurance, accessories; Amar Autos]

convention only: in most Hindi-speakers' pronunciation बॉल 'ball' does not have the 'aw' sound that it has in English, but sounds like the vowel in the word 'calm'. The sign has no standard Roman transliteration, but is here transliterated as *â*:

बॉल	*bâl*	ball
मॉडर्न	*mâḍarn*	modern
सॉरी	*sârī*	sorry

Fig 17: What kind of shop is this?

Many English words are quite awkward to write in Devanagari, particularly because of their frequent consonant clusters and dipththongs:

इंस्ट्रक्शन	*instṛakśan*	instruction
अकाउंटेंट	*akāunṭenṭ*	accountant

Exercise 17

Transcribe the following into the original English:

टेल मी नाट इन मोर्नफुल नंबर्ज़,
    लाइफ़ इज़ बट ऐन एम्प्टी ड्रीम;
फार द सोल इज़ डेड दैट स्लंबर्ज़,
    एंड थिंग्ज़ आर नाट वाट दे सीम।

[Answer: Modern Jewellers.]

The verse in the exercise above shows some typical features of English in Devanagari: the use of retroflex consonants for the English 't', 'd'; the different 'o' sounds of 'not' and 'for' both being assimilated to *ā* (the optional ऑ *â* form has not been used here); the use of consecutive vowels to represent diphthongs such as that in 'life' (लाइफ़ *lāif*); the use of द् *d* and थ् *th* for voiced and unvoiced 'th' (in 'the' and 'things' respectively).

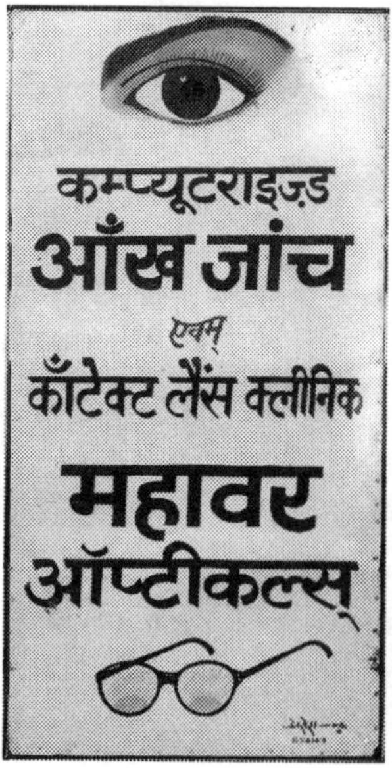

Fig 18: आँख जांच, *on the right, means 'eye testing';* व *(on the left) and* एवम् *(on the right) both mean 'and'. The rest of the text here is mostly in English. What are the names of the two businesses advertised, and what services do they offer?*

Among other problems in writing English in Devanagari, there is no adequate way of showing the soft *j* sound in the word 'vision', which has to be written either as विझन *vijhan* or as विज़न *vizan.* (Many speakers weaken the consonant almost to a 'y' sound, saying *'viyan, leyar'* for 'vision, leisure'.)

[Answer: (left) Imperial Barber Shop – Ladies and Gents Beauty Parlour, Bridal Make-up and Beautician Course; (right) Mahāvar Opticals –computerised eye testing and contact lens clinic .]

While words borrowed from English will have retroflex consonants, loanwords from (or influenced by) Portuguese, with its softer consonants, have dentals: बोतल *botal*, 'bottle', represents Portuguese 'botelha'. If the Portuguese traders had been less successful in the ventures on the western seaboard of India in the early colonial period, India would probably have an 'English' bottle, spelled with a retroflex ट *ṭa*! Portuguese influence is also seen in the month names. A complete list of the twelve months gives good reading practice – but the sequence has been muddled up for you here, just in case things get too easy.

दिसंबर	मई	फ़रवरी
मार्च	जुलाई	अगस्त
जनवरी	अप्रैल	नवंबर
अक्तूबर	जून	सितंबर

As with many other English loanwords in Hindi, the gender of the month names depends on their endings: those that end in *-ī* (like जनवरी *janvarī*) are feminine, the rest are masculine. There's more information on gender coming up on page 86.

UNIT 8
More about Hindi words and spellings

Some dog-fights over conjunct forms

The way in which conjunct consonants are printed, typed and written varies a great deal depending on habit and the available technologies, and we have already seen how some conjuncts (such as *śva*, written श्व or श्‍व, or *nna*, written न्न or न्‍न) have more than one form.

The limited keyboard of a conventional typewriter cannot produce the full range of conjunct forms; for example, typewriters that cannot produce त्त (*tta*) have to make do with त्‍त – hardly satisfactory for general use, as it can all too easily be confused with ल. Unfortunately, some attempted 'standardisation' of forms occurred in the decades before computers removed all such limitations of keyboard layout; so there is official backing for such awkward forms as our example त्‍त, allowing such spellings as कुत्‍ता and कलकत्‍ता rather than insisting on the much more elegant कुत्ता and कलकत्ता.

The standardising authorities have also condemned such clear and elegant conjunct forms as द्य for *dya* (preferring द्‌य) and द्ध for *ddha* (preferring द्‌ध); and they even recommend that an *i*-sign in a syllable such as *ddhi* should fall *between* the two components of the conjunct, giving द्‌धि instead of the well-established द्धि ! The resulting बुद्‌धिमानी *buddhimānī* ('wisdom') is a strange and inelegant form of बुद्धिमानी; but fortunately, Hindi's wiser public ignores such official recommendations and sticks to the old forms that have served so well for centuries.

Exercise 18

Identify these geographical names:

भारत	गुजरात	बिहार	ढाका	इलाहाबाद
तमिल नाडु	लखनऊ	कराची	लाहौर	देहरा दून
नेपाल	मसूरी	मथुरा	कोटा	वाराणसी
बनारस	यमुना	हिमालय	केरल	उड़ीसा

Fig 20: Where is bus 402 coming from (on the left) and going to (on the right)?

Where does Hindi vocabulary come from?

The basic stock of Hindi vocabulary comes from various sources. The most important categories are:

1. *Tatsama* words: loanwords from Sanskrit, complete with the original Sanskrit spellings. (The term 'tatsama' means 'same as that', where 'that' refers to Sanskrit.) Examples are विकसित *vikăsit,* 'developed' (whose *-it* participle ending, equivalent to the '-ed' of the English participle, is found in many such words), राजधानी *rājdhānī,* 'capital city', and कृपा *kṛpā,* 'kindness, grace'. Many Sanskrit words have changed their meanings and contexts of use in the modern Hindi

[Answer: Aukhlā Gā̃v (Okhla village); Jāmā Masjid (Friday Mosque). Many place names are rather unstable in their spellings: ओखला is more common than औखला.]

setting. For example, the original sense of आकाशवाणी *ākāśvāṇī* is 'voice from heaven, oracle', but it now names the Indian radio service; as a term for 'radio' generally it cannot, however, compete with the loanword रेडियो *reḍiyo,* which is well-established in Hindi.

2. *Tadbhava* words: words that have evolved organically from Sanskrit and Prakrit, i.e. medieval and modern derivatives of ancient words. (The term 'tadbhava' means 'of the nature of that'.) Having been subject to erosion over centuries of use, tadbhava are usually reduced versions of their originals: thus Hindi सात *sāt,* 'seven', derives from Sanskrit सप्त *sapta,* typically compensating for the reduced conjunct with a lengthened vowel. A less obvious example is Hindi ढाई *ḍhāī,*'two and a half', whose Sanskrit original अर्धतृतीय *ardhatṛtīya,* 'half [less than] three', has been heavily eroded over time. Words that have a simple shape in their tatsama forms hardly change, if at all: नाम *nām,* 'name', is both tatsama and tadbhava – i.e. both Sanskrit and Hindi – because even the heavy use of centuries cannot simplify an already simple word.

   Tatsama and tadbhava versions of the same word may co-exist in Hindi, sometimes with a difference in meaning: tatsama कर्म *karmă* means 'karma, action whose fruits are enjoyed in later lives', whereas its tadbhava derivative काम *kām* is the everyday word for 'work'; and tatsama क्षेत्र *kṣetră means* 'field' in an abstract sense ('field of knowledge' etc.), whereas its tadbhava derivative खेत *khet* is a field you can plough. In these two examples we see again the reduction of the final conjunct.

3. Neologisms: new words formed from Sanskrit roots. Just as European languages developed and modernised by forming new vocabulary from Latin and Greek roots, Hindi has formed many words from the inexhaustible stocks of Sanskrit. But whereas the European languages

gradually developed new vocabularies to cope with new technologies and concepts as they came into being over several centuries, Indian languages were thrown in at the deep end when these technologies and concepts were brought to India ready-made by the colonial powers. So Indian languages have first had to translate, and then compete with, English loanwords such as 'radio' and 'train'. Unsurprisingly, the new Indian coinings have had a tough time in taking the place of their well-established English synonyms: we have already seen how रेडियो *reḍiyo* has become a Hindi word. Similarly the word ट्रेन *ṭren,* 'train', runs everywhere, whereas the infamous coining लोह्-पथ-गामिनी *loh-path-gāminī,* 'iron-path-traveller', never made it out of the station. Many neologisms are calques – literal word-by-word translations, usually from the English; thus दूरदर्शन *dūrdarśan,* 'television', the name of the government TV channel in India, is composed of the two Sanskrit elements दूर *dūr,* 'distant' (for Greek-derived 'tele') and दर्शन *darśan* 'vision' (for Latin-derived 'vision') – but most people are happy just to say टी-वी *ṭī-vī* 'TV' !

4. Loanwords from Persian, and through Persian from Arabic and Turkish. These have formed a vital part of the Hindi language for centuries (although in recent times there has been a move to replace them with Sanskritic words as part of a general 'Hinduisation' of Indian culture, forcing a more literal division between the complementary sister-languages of Hindi and Urdu); the natural state of Hindi is that of a mixed language, accommodating words from many different sources, and this mixture gives it strength and subtlety. Common Hindi words from Perso-Arabic sources are बाद *bād,* 'afterwards', कुरसी *kursī,* 'chair', मकान *makān,* 'house' and तबला *tablā,* 'tabla' (all Arabic in origin); and कि *ki,* 'that' (as a conjunction), जानवर *jānvar,* 'animal', सब्ज़ी *sabzī,* 'vegetable', बाज़ार *bāzār,* 'market', सितार *sitār,* 'sitar', and सरकार *sarkār,* 'government' (all Persian).

5. Loanwords from English and Portuguese. We have seen many of these earlier in the book. English words are flooding, not to say drowning, the Hindi language, with कार *kār*, किचन *kican* and बाथरूम *bāthrūm* in danger of ousting their equivalents गाड़ी *gāṛī*, रसोईघर *rasoīghar*, गुसलख़ाना *gusal<u>kh</u>ānā*. These days one frequently hears such sentences as क्या साइड-स्ट्रीट में यू-टर्न एलाउड है ? *kyā sāiḍ-sṭrīṭ mẽ yū-ṭarn elāuḍ hai?* 'Is a U-turn allowed in a side-street?'. By contrast, Portuguese influence is a historical one only – i.e. it is no longer contributing new words to Hindi; but it accounts for many everyday items such as कमरा *kamrā* 'room', अलमारी *almārī* 'cupboard', इस्तरी *istrī* 'an iron', and मिस्तरी *mistrī* 'mechanic, skilled worker'.

Fig 21: Can you find eight different English loanwords in this shop sign?

Gender in Hindi

Every Hindi noun has a gender – either masculine or feminine. Some adjectives (and verbs) reflect these genders. The characteristic masculine ending is -*ā*, contrasted with feminine -*ī*; thus लंबा लड़का *lambā laṛkā*,

[Answer: You can **book** a **coffee machine** at Shiv **Traders**, **pho[ne]** 211134; **birthday cakes** and all birthday provisions available at reasonable **rates**.]

'tall boy', लंबी लड़की *lambī laṛkī,* 'tall girl'. Adjectives that do not end in *-ā / -ī* have no way of showing agreement: होशियार लड़का *hośiyār laṛkā,* 'clever boy', होशियार लड़की, *hośiyār laṛkī,* 'clever girl'.

In the example of लड़का *laṛkā* / लड़की *laṛkī,* grammatical gender obviously follows sexual gender; but there is no such clearcut principle for inanimate nouns such as घर *ghar,* 'house', which happens to be masculine, or मेज़ *mez,* 'table', which happens to be feminine; so when you learn a new noun it's a good idea to learn its gender also.

Sometimes, the gender of a noun can be inferred from its form: the '*-ā / -ī*' masculine/feminine pattern of लड़का / लड़की is very common, with examples like कमरा *kamrā,* 'room', डिब्बा *ḍibbā,* 'box', and कपड़ा *kapṛā,* 'cloth' all being masculine, and बिजली *bijlī,* 'elecricity', रोशनी *rośnī,* 'light' and बत्ती *battī,* 'lamp, light' all feminine. Place-names follow suit: those ending *-ā* are masculine (आगरा *āgrā,* कलकत्ता *kalkattā*), those ending *-ī* are feminine (दिल्ली *dillī,* वाराणसी *vārāṇasī*). And all rivers are feminine, like the word नदी *nadī,* 'river', itself.

Stress in Varanasi: while most Westerners pronounce the place name वाराणसी with a stress on the third syllable ('Varanási'), this is actually the one and only *short* syllable in the entire word, and therefore bears *less* stress than its neighbours. Stress is generally much more even in Hindi than it is in English; and getting it right is essential to good pronunciation. (The name बनारस *banāras,* incidentally, is an old-established derivative of वाराणसी; and a third name for this ancient city is काशी *kāśī,* 'the luminous', or, more romantically, 'City of Light'.)

There are many exceptions to this '*-ā / -ī*' rule or tendency: पानी *pānī,* 'water' and आदमी *ādmī,* 'man' both end in *-ī* but are masculine, while आशा *āśā,* 'hope' and भाषा *bhāṣā,* 'language' both end in *-ā* but are feminine. These last two belong to a large group of loanwords from Sanskrit, where -ā is a feminine ending: many girls' names, such as उषा 'Usha' and रेणुका 'Renuka' end in *-ā,* and these are all Sanskritic. And all languages are feminine, like the word भाषा *bhāṣā*, 'language', itself.

Hindi borrows several Sanskrit abstract nouns ending in *-tā*, which means '-ness', etc: गंभीरता *gambhīrtā*, 'seriousness', मधुरता *madhurtā*, 'sweetness',साक्षरता *sākṣartā*, 'literacy', and सुंदरता *sundartā*, 'beauty'. Being Sanskrit nouns ending in *-ā*, these are all feminine.

Hindi verb stems used as abstract nouns are feminine: समझ *samajh*, 'understanding', पहुँच *pahũc*, 'reach', दौड़ *dauṛ* 'running, race' and खीझ *khījh*, 'irritation' are from the verbs समझना *samajhnā*, 'to understand, पहुँचना *pahũcnā*, 'to reach', दौड़ना *dauṛnā* 'to run' and खीझना *khījhnā*, 'to be irritated' respectively.

English '-ing' words are often borrowed in Hindi, and these too are feminine: शूटिंग *śūṭing*, '(film-)shooting', मीटिंग *mīṭing*, 'meeting' and ड्राइंग *ḍrāing*, 'drawing' are common examples.

Other loanwords from English may take the gender of a Hindi synonym or other associated word: thus कार *kār* is feminine, like गाड़ी *gāṛī*; and बियर *biyar* 'beer') too is feminine, like शराब *śarāb* 'alcoholic drink, booze'.

One of the reasons why it's so important to know a noun's gender is that gender determines the way in which the noun is made plural. Here are the basic principles:

	SINGULAR	PLURAL
Most masculine nouns that end in *-ā* change to *-e*	कमरा room	कमरे rooms
	लड़का boy	लड़के boys
Other masculine nouns don't change	आदमी man	आदमी men
	घर house	घर houses
Feminine nouns that end in *-ī* change to *-iyā̃*	बत्ती light	बत्तियाँ lights
	लड़की girl	लड़कियाँ girls
Other feminine nouns add *-ẽ*	मेज़ table	मेज़ें tables
	तस्वीर picture	तस्वीरें pictures

Notice that आदमी *ādmī* can mean both 'man' and 'men'. The number may become apparent in an -*ā* adjective, which changes to -*e* in the plural: मोटा आदमी *moṭā ādmī,* 'fat man', मोटे आदमी *moṭe ādmī,* 'fat men'. Only masculine -*ā* adjectives change like this, all others stay the same. Look at the following examples and notice which nouns and which adjectives change in the plural:

MASCULINE	बड़ा कमरा big room	बड़े कमरे big rooms
	बड़ा मकान big house	बड़े मकान big houses
	लाल पत्थर red stone	लाल पत्थर red stones
FEMININE	छोटी बेटी little daughter	छोटी बेटियाँ little daughters
	बड़ी आँख big eye	बड़ी आँखें big eyes
	साफ़ मेज़ clean table	साफ़ मेज़ें clean tables

राष्ट्रीय
सहारा 2
नयी दिल्ली, मंगलवार, 25 जनवरी, 2000

ग्लोबल डायरी

चेचन्या ने अफगानिस्तान में दूतावास खोला

काबुल, (रायटर)। चेचन्या ने अफगानिस्तान में रविवार को अपना दूतावास खोल लिया। काबुल में शहर के फ्लावर स्ट्रीट में एक इमारत पर चेचेन ध्वज फहरा रहा है। अफगानिस्तान की तालिबान सरकार चेचेन अलगाववादियों को एक सरकार के रूप में मान्यता देने वाली विश्व की पहली सरकार है। इस बीच चेचन्या में रूसी सेना द्वारा गोलीबारी जारी है। दूतावास का उद्घाटन अफगानिस्तान के विदेश उपमंत्री अब्दुल रहमान ने किया। तालिबान अधिकारियों ने रूसी सेना के खिलाफ जारी चेचेन संघर्ष की प्रशंसा करते हुए अन्य मुस्लिम देशों से उनका समर्थन करने का अनुरोध किया है। तालिबान ने चेचेन विद्रोहियों को हरसंभव सहायता देने का वादा किया है। इससे पहले पिछले सप्ताह तालिबान

Fig 22: Where and when was this newspaper published? And which two countries feature in the headline of this 'Global Diary' section?

[Answer: New Delhi, 25 January 2000 (मंगलवार *mangalvār* is 'Tuesday'); the countries referred to are Chechnya and Afghanistan, the latter name being written without the two dots that a full spelling would require – अफ़ग़ानिस्तान.]

APPENDIXES

APPENDIX 1

Examples of Hindi handwriting

एक दिन मेरी छोटी बेटी ने पूछा, 'मम्मी, पुलिस आदमी होता है या औरत ?'। क्योंकि इस छोटी-सी उम्र में उसने अधिकतर पुरुष पुलिस को ही देखा था, सो मैंने कह दिया कि आदमी होता है। उसी वक़्त दूसरा सवाल उठा, 'तो फिर हम क्यों कहते हैं कि "पुलिस आ गई", "पुलिस आ गया" क्यों नहीं कहते ?'

Translation: One day my little daughter asked, 'Mummy, are the police men or women?'. Because at this young age she had mostly seen *male* police, I said 'men'. Immediately another question came up, 'So then why do we say "The police have come [feminine]", why don't we say "the police have come [masculine]" ?'

[The Hindi word पुलिस *pulis* has feminine gender, which it has probably acquired from related Hindi words such as फ़ौज *fauj* and सेना *senā* 'army'. It is used in the singular.]

Example 1

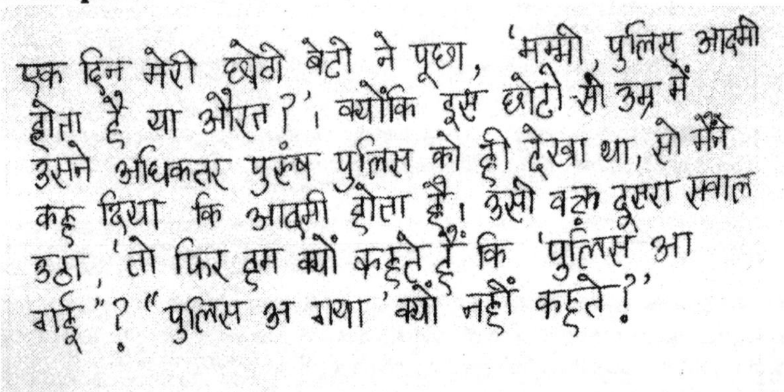
एक दिन मेरी छोटी बेटी ने पूछा, 'मम्मी, पुलिस आदमी
होता है या औरत ?'। क्योंकि इस छोटी-सी उम्र में
उसने अधिकतर पुरुष पुलिस को ही देखा था, सो मैंने
कह दिया कि आदमी होता है। उसी वक़्त दूसरा सवाल
उठा, 'तो फिर हम क्यों कहते हैं कि "पुलिस आ
गई"? "पुलिस आ गया" क्यों नहीं कहते?'

Example 2

एक दिन मेरी छोटी बेटी ने पूछा, 'मम्मी, पुलिस
आदमी होता है या औरत?' क्योंकि इस छोटी-सी
उम्र में उसने अधिकतर पुरुष पुलिस को
ही देखा था, सो मैंने कह दिया कि आदमी होता है।
उसी वक़्त दूसरा सवाल उठा, 'तो फिर हम
क्यों कहते हैं कि "पुलिस आ गई"?
"पुलिस आ गया" क्यों नहीं कहते?'

Example 3

एक दिन मेरी छोटी बेटी ने पूछा, 'मम्मी,
पुलिस आदमी होता है या औरत?' क्योंकि
इस छोटी-सी उम्र में उसने अधिकतर
पुरुष पुलिस को ही देखा था, सो मैंने
कह दिया कि आदमी होता है। उसी
वक़्त दूसरा सवाल उठा, 'तो फिर हम
क्यों कहते हैं कि "पुलिस आ गई"?
"पुलिस आ गया" क्यों नहीं कहते?'

Example 4

एक दिन मेरी छोटी बेटी ने पूछा,
"मम्मी, पुलिस आदमी होता है या
औरत?" क्योंकि इस छोटी-सी
उम्र में उसने अधिकतर पुरुष
पुलिस को ही देखा था, सो मैंने
कह दिया कि आदमी होता है। उसी
वक़्त दूसरा सवाल उठा, "तो फिर
हम क्यों कहते हैं कि "पुलिस आ
गई"? "पुलिस आ गया" क्यों नहीं
कहते?

Example 5

एक दिन मेरी छोटी बेटी ने पूछा, 'मम्मी, पुलिस
आदमी होता है या औरत?'। क्योंकि इस
छोटी-सी उम्र में उसने अधिकतर पुरुष पुलिस
को ही देखा था, सो मैंने कह दिया कि आदमी
होता है। उसी वक़्त दूसरा सवाल उठा, 'तो
फिर हम क्यों कहते हैं कि "पुलिस आ गई"?
"पुलिस आ गया" क्यों नहीं कहते?'

Example 6

एक दिन मेरी छोटी बेटी ने पूछा 'मम्मी,
पुलिस आदमी होता है या औरत?'।
क्योंकि इस छोटी-सी उम्र में उसने
अधिकतर पुरुष पुलिस को ही देखा था,
सो मैंने कह दिया कि आदमी होता है।
उसी वक्त दूसरा सवाल उठा, 'तो फिर
हम क्यों कहते हैं कि "पुलिस आ
गई"? "पुलिस आ गया"
क्यों नहीं कहते?'

APPENDIX 2

Minimal pairs

This section gives you further practice in the spelling and pronunciation of pairs of words that are identical in all but one feature. If at all possible, try to get a Hindi-speaker to read out (or even better, record) the list for you; it will be a great help in getting your ear accustomed to the sounds of Hindi.

Words that are translated '(to)...', such as 'बदल (to) change' are verb stems (see p. 47); add - ना for the infinitive (e.g. बदलना).

Vowels

अ/आ *a / ā*

दम^{m}	breath, life	दाम^{m}	price
मन^{m}	mind, heart	मान^{m}	pride
बल^{m}	force	बाल^{m}	hair
भरत^{m}	Bharat	भारत^{m}	India
पर	on; but	पार	across
दस	ten	दास^{m}	slave
गई	went^{f}	गाई	sang^{f}
कल	yesterday; tomorrow	काल^{m}	time, Time
कम	little, less	काम^{m}	work
बदल	(to) change	बादल^{m}	cloud
कमल^{m}	lotus	कमाल^{m}	miracle
नई	new^{f}	नाई^{m}	barber

इ/ई *i/ī*

सिख m	Sikh	सीख f	instruction
मिल m	mill	मील m	mile
दिन m	day	दीन m	poor; religion
भिड़ f	hornet	भीड़ f	crowd
दिया	gave	दीया m	oil lamp
सिल f	grinding stone	सील f	dampness
पिटना	to be beaten	पीटना	to beat
जाति f	caste	जाती	going f

उ/ऊ *u/ū*

उन	them	ऊन f	wool
धुल	(to) be washed	धूल f	dust
पुरा m	quarter of town	पूरा	complete, full
फुट m	foot	फूट	(to) burst
घुस	(to) enter, sneak in	घूस f	bribe
कुल m	family; total	कूल m	bank of river, pond
सुख m	happiness	सूख	(to) dry
सुना	heard	सूना	deserted, empty

एए/ऐ *e / ai*

मेला m	fair	मैला	dirty
में	in	मैं	I
देव m	god	दैव	divine
चेत m	consciousness	चैत m	name of a month
फेल	fail, failed	फैल	(to) spread
हे	Oh!	है	is
सेर m	a weight of about 1kg	सैर f	excursion
बेल m	wood-apple	बैल m	bullock

ओ/औ *o / au*

ओर f	direction	और	and
सो	so	सौ	hundred
जो	the one who	जौ m	barley
डोल m	rocking	डौल m	shape, form
बोर	bore, bored	बौर m	mango blossom
खोल	(to) open	खौल	(to) boil
कोर f	edge, tip	कौर m	mouthful of food
लोटना	to roll, sprawl	लौटना	to return

on-nasal / nasal

बास^{m}	fragrance	बाँस^{m}	bamboo
गई	went^{f}	गईं	went$^{f.pl}$
पाई	obtained^{f}	पाईं	obtained$^{f.pl}$
करे	may do	करें	may do^{pl}
लड़को	(O) boys!	लड़कों	(to, from) boys
पूछ	(to) ask	पूँछ^{f}	tail
हा	ah!	हाँ	yes
है	is	हैं	are

onsonants

ingle / double

बचा	saved, survived	बच्चा^{m}	child
सन^{m}	hemp	सन्न	numbed
समान	equal	सम्मान	respect
बटा	divided	बट्टा^{m}	rebate
चुनी	chose^{f}	चुन्नी^{f}	scarf
पता^{m}	address	पत्ता^{m}	leaf
बला^{f}	calamity	बल्ला^{m}	beam, pole
सटा	stuck, joined	सट्टा^{m}	transaction

सता	(to) torment	सत्ता [f]	power
पका	cooked	पक्का	ripe, firm

The word पक्का has a wide range of meanings, mostly to do with thoroughness or permanence: पक्की सड़क 'a *metalled* road'; पक्का मकान 'a *brick-built* house'; पक्का इरादा 'a *firm* intention'; पक्का बदमाश 'an *utter* villain'.

Non-retroflex / retroflex

आता	comes	आटा [m]	flour
ताल [m]	musical time	टाल	(to) postpone
तीन	three	टीन [m]	tin
छोर [m]	edge	छोड़	(to) leave
सरक	(to) slip, creep	सड़क [f]	road, street
घात [f]	stratagem	घाट [m]	riverbank
सारी	whole, entire [f]	साड़ी [m]	sari

Non-aspirated / aspirated

बाड़ [f]	fence	बाढ़ [f]	flood
गाता	singing	गाथा [f]	ballad
गंद [m]	stench	गंध [f]	fragrance
बंद	closed	बंध [m]	embankment, bund

चलना	to move	छलना	to deceive
चना ^{m}	chickpea	छना	sifted, strained
चोर ^{m}	thief	छोर ^{m}	edge, border
जूठा	despoiled by touch	झूठा	false
कुल ^{m}	family, dynasty	खुल	(to) open
मोड़ा	turned	मोढ़ा ^{m}	bamboo stool
पाट ^{m}	board	पाठ ^{m}	recitation
पल ^{m}	moment	फल ^{m}	fruit
टीका ^{m}	forehead-mark	ठीका, ठेका ^{m}	contract
संग ^{m}	association	संघ ^{m}	union; sect
ताली ^{f}	clapping	थाली ^{f}	platter
ताना ^{m}	taunt	थाना ^{m}	police station
तक	until, up to	थक	(to) tire
डाल ^{f}	branch	ढाल ^{m}	incline

Other contrasts

हँस	(to) laugh	हंस ^{m}	goose, swan
खाना ^{m}	food; to eat	ख़ाना ^{m}	room, place
सीख ^{f}	instruction	सीख़ ^{f}	skewer

APPENDIX 3

Reading practice

PART ONE These reading sentences consist of simple questions and statements of the kind that were introduced in Unit 5. All the vocabulary is given in the Glossary, and most of it has already occurred in the units themselves. The transliteration of each sentence is printed on the opposite page, and an English translation follows at the end, so you can test both your reading and your comprehension.

१ क्या यह किताब सस्ती है ?

२ जी हाँ, काफ़ी सस्ती है ।

३ क्या लाहौर हिन्दुस्तान में है ?

४ जी नहीं, लाहौर पाकिस्तान में है ।

५ क्या अमृतसर पंजाब में है ?

६ जी हाँ, अमृतसर पंजाब में है ।

७ अमृतसर हिन्दुस्तान में है । मगर वह लाहौर से दूर नहीं है ।

८ क्या तुम हिन्दुस्तानी हो ?

९ नहीं, मैं हिन्दुस्तानी नहीं हूँ, मैं श्री लंका से हूँ ।

१० क्या "टीच योरसेल्फ़ बिगिनर्स हिन्दी स्क्रिप्ट" में तस्वीरें हैं ?

११ जी हाँ, कई तस्वीरें हैं ।

१२ ये नई तस्वीरें काफ़ी अच्छीं हैं ।

१३ ताज कहाँ है ?

१४ ताज महल आगरे में है पर ताज होटल मुंबई में है ।

1 kyā yah kitāb sastī hai?

2 jī hā̃, kāfī sastī hai.

3 kyā lāhaur hindustān mẽ hai?

4 jī nahī̃, lāhaur pākistān mẽ hai.

5 kyā amr̥tsar panjāb mẽ hai?

6 jī hā̃, amr̥tsar panjāb mẽ hai.

7 amr̥tsar hindustān mẽ hai. magar vah lāhaur se dūr nahī̃ hai.

8 kyā tum hindustānī ho ?

9 nahī̃, maĩ hindustānī nahī̃ hū̃, maĩ śrī lankā se hū̃.

10 kyā *ṭīc yorself biginars hindī skripṭ* mẽ tasvīrẽ haĩ?

11 jī hā̃, kaī tasvīrẽ haĩ.

12 ye naī tasvīrẽ kāfī acchī haĩ.

13 taj kahā̃ hai?

14 tāj mahal āgre mẽ hai magar tāj hoṭal mumbaī mẽ hai.

१५ क्या आगरा वाराणसी से बहुत दूर है ?

१६ जी हाँ, वाराणसी काफ़ी दूर है ।

१७ तुम कौन हो ? और यह लड़का कौन है ?

१८ मैं उषा हूँ । और यह लड़का दिनेश है ।

१९ क्या देवनागरी लिपि पुरानी है ?

२० जी हाँ, देवनागरी बहुत पुरानी है ।

२१ रसोईघर में क्या है ?

२२ रसोईघर में तीन कुरसियाँ और एक मेज़ है ।

२३ मेज़ पर क्या है ?

२४ मेज़ पर चीनी, गाजर और दूध है ।

२५ संगीता और सुहास कहाँ हैं ?

२६ उषा जी और रेणुका देहरा दून में हैं ।

२७ क्या देहरा दून हिमाचल प्रदेश में है ?

२८ जी नहीं, देहरा दून उत्तर प्रदेश में है ।

२९ क्या वह बड़ी नदी यमुना है ?

३० जी नहीं, वह गंगा है । यमुना यहाँ से दूर है ।

३१ क्या भगवद्गीता संस्कृत में है ?

३२ जी हाँ, पर यह पुरानी किताब हिन्दी में है ।

३३ क्या यह दाम ठीक है ?

15 kyā āgrā vārāṇasī se bahut dūr hai?

16 jī hā̃, vārāṇasī kāfī dūr hai.

17 tum kaun ho? aur yah laṛkā kaun hai?

18 maĩ uṣā hū̃. aur yah laṛkā dineś hai.

19 kyā devanāgrī lipi purānī hai ?

20 jī hā̃, devanāgrī bahut purānī hai.

21 rasoīghar mẽ kyā hai?

22 rasoīghar mẽ tīn kursiyā̃ aur ek mez hai.

23 mez par kyā hai?

24 mez par cīnī, gājar aur dūdh hai.

25 sangītā aur suhās kahā̃ haĩ?

26 sangītā aur suhās dehrā dūn mẽ haĩ.

27 kyā dehrā dūn himācal pradeś mẽ hai?

28 jī nahī̃, dehrā dūn uttar pradeś mẽ hai.

29 kyā vah baṛī nadī yamunā hai?

30 jī nahī̃, vah gangā hai. yamunā yahā̃ se dūr hai.

31 kyā bhagvadgītā sanskṛt mẽ hai?

32 jī hā̃, par yah purānī kitāb hindī mẽ hai.

33 kyā yah dām ṭhīk hai?

३४ जी नहीं, यह बहुत महँगा है।

३५ क्या युनिवर्सिटी आज बंद है ?

३६ जी हाँ, आज छुट्टी है, और विश्वविद्यालय बंद है।

३७ आप लोग कैसे हैं ?

३८ धन्यवाद, हम ठीक हैं।

३९ यह नई किताब पढ़िए, यह बहुत अच्छी है।

४० यह फल खाइए, यह बहुत ताज़ा है।

४१ यह गाना सुनिए, यह बहुत मीठा है।

४२ वह नई फ़िल्म देखिए, बुरी नहीं है।

४३ आज पिताजी और चाचाजी कहाँ हैं ?

४४ वे आज यहाँ नहीं हैं। दोनों बाहर हैं।

४५ ऋषि और राज कहाँ हैं ?

४६ वे दोनों रसोईघर में हैं।

४७ प्रताप कौन है ? क्या वह नौकर है ?

४८ जी नहीं, वह नौकर नहीं है, वह विद्यार्थी है।

४९ दीवाली कब है ?

५० दीवाली कल है।

५१ कल छुट्टी है। तुम यहाँ आओ न ?

५२ वह दूसरी किताब क्या है ?

५३ यह किताब "टीच योरसेल्फ़ हिन्दी" है।

34 jī nahī̃, yah bahut mahãgā hai.

35 kyā yunivarsiṭī āj band hai?

36 jī hã̄, āj chuṭṭī hai, aur viśvăvidyālay band hai.

37 āp log kaise haĩ?

38 dhanyavād, ham ṭhīk haĩ.

39 yah naī kitāb paṛhie, yah bahut acchī hai.

40 yah phal khāie, yah bahut tāzā hai.

41 yah gānā sunie, yah bahut mīṭhā hai.

42 vah naī film dekhie, burī nahī̃ hai.

43 āj pitājī aur cācājī kahā̃ haĩ?

44 ve āj yahā̃ nahī̃ haĩ. donõ bāhar haĩ.

45 ṛṣi aur rāj kahā̃ haĩ?

46 ve donõ rasoīghar mẽ haĩ.

47 pratāp kaun hai? kyā vah naukar hai?

48 jī nahī̃, vah naukar nahī̃ hai, vah vidyārthī hai.

49 dīvālī kab hai?

50 dīvālī kal hai.

51 kal chuṭṭī hai. tum yahā̃ āo na?

52 vah dūsrī kitāb kyā hai?

53 yah kitāb 'ṭīc yorself hindī' hai.

Translation of the PART ONE sentences.

1 Is this book cheap?

2 Yes, [it] is quite cheap.

3 Is Lahore in India?

4 No, Lahore is in Pakistan.

5 Is Amritsar in Panjab?

6 Yes, Amritsar is in Panjab.

7 Amritsar is in India. But it's not far from Lahore.

8 Are you Indian?

9 No, I'm not Indian, I'm from Sri Lanka.

10 Are there pictures in *Teach Yourself Beginner's Hindi Script*?

11 Yes, there are several pictures.

12 These new pictures are quite good.

13 Where is the Taj?

14 The Taj Mahal is in Agra but the Taj hotel is in Mumbai.

15 Is Agra very far from Varanasi?

16 Yes, Varanasi is quite far away.

17 Who are you? And who's this boy?

18 I am Usha. And this boy is Dinesh.

19 Is the Devanagari script old?

20 Yes, Devanagari is very old.

21 What is there in the kitchen?

22 There's a table and three chairs in the kitchen.

23 What is there on the table?

24 There's sugar, carrots and milk on the table.

25 Where are Sangeeta and Suhas?

26 Sangeeta and Suhas are in Dehra Dun.

27 Is Dehra Dun in Himachal Pradesh?

28 No, Dehra Dun is in Uttar Pradesh.

29 Is that big river the Yamuna?

30 No, that's the Ganga (Ganges). The Yamuna is far from here.

31 Is the *Bhagavadgītā* in Sanskrit?

32 Yes, but this old book is in Hindi.

33 Is this price correct?

34 No, this is very expensive.

35 Is the university closed today?

36 Yes, today's a holiday, and the university's closed.

37 How are you people?

38 Thank you, we're fine.

39 Read this new book, it's very good.

40 Eat this fruit, it's very fresh.

41 Listen to this song, it's very sweet.

42 See that new film, [it's] not bad.

43 Where are Father and Uncle today?

44 They're not here today. [They're] both out.

45 Where are Rishi and Raj?

46 They're both in the kitchen.

47 Who is Pratap? Is he a servant?

48 No, he's not a servant, he's a student.

49 When is Diwali?

50 Diwali is tomorrow.

51 Tomorrow is a holiday. Come here, won't you?

52 What's that other book?

53 This other book is *Teach Yourself Hindi.*

PART TWO This story is meant as reading practice for those who are already familiar with spoken Hindi and are using this book to add a knowledge of the script. Vocabulary for this story is *not* given in the glossary, but a translation follows at the end.

सुन्दरलाल उर्फ़ ...

हमारे शहर में एक लड़का रहता था जिसका नाम था सुन्दरलाल। वह शायद पंद्रह सोलह साल का था। सुन्दरलाल असल में सुन्दर बिलकुल नहीं था, काफ़ी बदसूरत था। इस वजह से स्कूल में सारे बच्चे उसे चिढ़ाते थे और गालियाँ दिया करते थे। सुन्दरलाल अपने माँ-बाप से शिकायत करता रहता था कि "मुझे इतना बेकार नाम क्यों दिया गया। दुनिया में अच्छे नामों की कोई कमी है क्या ? मुझे रामलाल या कृष्ण कुमार जैसा कोई साधारण नाम क्यों नहीं दिया गया ?" पर उसकी बात कौन सुनता। उसके पिता को उससे बात करने का समय भी नहीं था; वे तो अपनी दुकान को चलाने में हमेशा व्यस्त रहते थे। और जब कभी सुन्दरलाल अपनी माता से अपने नाम के बारे में कुछ कहने लगता तो वे बोलतीं, "अरे बेटे चुप भी कर, मुझे अपना काम करने दे, तुझे क्या मालूम इन बातों के बारे में।"

एक दिन अख़बार पढ़ते वक़्त सुन्दरलाल के मन में एक नई बात आई। कभी कभी ऐसा हो जाता है न, वह मन में कहने लगा, कि लोगों के नाम बदल दिए जाते हैं; मैं भी अपना नाम बदल लूँ तो अच्छा रहेगा। किसी दोस्त से पैसे लेकर उसने दिल्ली जानेवाली राजधानी एक्स्प्रेस के लिए टिकट लिया। उसने अपने घरवालों से कहा कि मैं अपने दोस्त ऋषि की बर्थडे पार्टी में जा रहा हूँ, दो दिन में लौटूँगा।

जिस दिन उसे दिल्ली जाना था उसने चोरी से रसोईघर में जाकर कुछ खाने की चीज़ें एक थैले में रख लीं। रात के साढ़े दस की ट्रेन थी; मगर सुन्दरलाल ने सोचा कि ट्रेन में इतनी भीड़ होगी कि देर से पहुँचनेवाले लोगों को सीट

sundarlāl urf...

hamāre śahar mẽ ek laṛkā rahtā thā jiskā nām thā sundarlāl. vah śāyad pandrah solah sāl kā thā. sundarlāl asal mẽ sundar bilkul nahī̃ thā, kāfī badsūrat thā. is vajah se skūl mẽ sāre bacce use ciṛhāte the aur gāliyā̃ diyā karte the. sundarlāl apne mā̃-bāp se śikāyat kartā rahtā thā ki 'mujhe itnā bekār nām kyõ diyā gayā. duniyā mẽ acche nāmõ kī koī kamī hai kyā? mujhe rāmlāl yā kṛṣṇă kumār jaisā koī sādhāraṇ nām kyõ nahī̃ diyā gayā?' par uskī bāt kaun suntā. uske pitā ko usse bāt karne kā samay bhī nahī̃ thā; ve to āpnī dukān ko calāne mẽ hameśā vyast rahte the. aur jab kabhī sundarlāl āpnī mātā se apne nām ke bāre mẽ kuch kahne lagtā to ve boltī̃, 'are beṭe cup bhī kar, mujhe apnā kām karne de, tujhe kyā mālūm in bātõ ke bāre mẽ'.

ek din a<u>kh</u>bār paṛhte vaqt sundarlāl ke man mẽ ek naī bāt āī. kabhī kabhī aisā ho jātā hai na, vah man mẽ kahne lagā, ki logõ ke nām badal die jāte haĩ; maĩ bhī apnā nām badal lū̃ to acchā rahegā. kisī dost se paise lekar usne dillī jānevālī rājdhānī ekspres ke lie ṭikaṭ liyā. usne apne gharvālõ se kahā ki maĩ apne dost ṛṣi kī barthḍe pārṭī mẽ jā rahā hū̃, do din mẽ lauṭū̃gā.

jis din use dillī jānā thā usne corī se rasoīghar mẽ jākar kuch khāne kī cīzẽ ek thaile mẽ rakh lī̃. rāt ke sāṛhe das kī ṭren thī; magar sundarlāl ne socā ki ṭren mẽ itnī bhīṛ hogī ki der se pahũcnevāle logõ ko sīṭ

पाने की कोई उम्मीद नहीं होगी, इसलिए वह ठीक नौ बजे घर से निकला। घर में उस वक़्त कोई भी न था, और सड़कें भी एकदम ख़ाली लग रही थीं। सुन्दरलाल के पास ज़्यादा पैसा नहीं था, इसलिए उसने निश्चय किया कि बस से स्टेशन नहीं जाना चाहिए, पैदल चलूँ तो किराये के पैसे बच जाएँगे। जब वह स्टेशन पहुँचा तो उसे बहुत आश्चर्य हुआ यह देखकर कि गाड़ी में बहुत-सी सीटें ख़ाली पड़ी थीं। उसे खिड़की के पास एक अच्छी-सी सीट मिल गई; और जैसे ही वह बर्थ पर बैठ गया उसकी आँख लग गई।

दो दिन बाद घर वापस आकर वह सोचने लगा कि माँ-बाप को कैसे बताऊँगा कि मैंने अपना नाम बदल लिया है। पिताजी कहेंगे कि तूने हमारे परिवार का नाम मिट्टी में मिला दिया है, और माँ न जाने क्या क्या कहेंगी।

सुबह का समय था। अपने कमरे का दरवाज़ा खोलकर वह ध्यान से सुनने लगा कि नीचे रसोईघर में क्या हो रहा है। उसके माँ-बाप नाश्ता करते हुए किसी पड़ोसी के लड़के की शादी के बारे में बातें कर रहे थे। जब सुन्दरलाल की माँ ने ज़ोर से चिल्लाकर कहा कि "सुन्दर, ओ सुन्दर, आ जा, तुझे देर हो जाएगी", तो सुन्दरलाल ने साहस बटोरकर जवाब दिया कि "माँ, मेरा नाम सुन्दर या सुन्दरलाल नहीं है। मैंने अपना नाम बदल लिया है। आज से मुझे 'एल्विस' कहा कीजिए।"

āne kī koī ummīd nahī̃ hogī, islie vah ṭhīk nau baje ghar se niklā. har mẽ us vaqt koī bhī na thā, aur saṛkẽ bhī ekdam khālī lag rahī thī̃. undarlāl ke pās zyādā paisā nahī̃ thā, islie usne niścay kiyā ki bas e sṭeśan nahī̃ jānā cāhie, paidal calū̃ to kirāye ke paise bac jāẽge. jab ah sṭeśan pahũcā to use bahut āścaryā huā yah dekhkar ki gāṛī mẽ ahut-sī sīṭẽ khālī paṛī thī̃. use khiṛkī ke pās ek acchī-sī sīṭ mil aī; aur jaise hī vah barth par baiṭh gayā uskī ā̃kh lag gaī.

o din bād ghar vāpas ākar vah socne lagā ki mā̃-bāp ko kaise batāū̃ga i maĩne apnā nām badal liyā hai. pitājī kahẽge ki tūne hamāre parivār kā ām miṭṭī mẽ milā diyā hai, aur mā̃ na jāne kyā kyā kahẽgī.

ubah kā samay thā. apne kamre kā darvāzā kholkar vah dhyān se sunne agā ki nīce rasoīghar mẽ kyā ho rahā hai. uske mā̃-bāp nāśtā karte hue isī paṛosī ke laṛke kī śādī ke bāre mẽ batẽ kar rahe the. jab sundarlāl ī mā̃ ne zor se cillākar kahā ki 'sundar, o sundar, ā jā, tujhe der ho āegī', to sundarlāl ne sāhas baṭorkar javāb diya ki 'mā̃, merā nām undar yā sundarlāl nahī̃ hai. maĩne āpna nām badal liyā hai. āj se mujhe elvis" kahā kījie'.

Translation of the PART TWO story.

Sundarlal alias...

In our town there lived a boy whose name was Sundarlal. He was mayb fifteen or sixteen years old. Sundarlal was in fact not handsome [*sunda* beautiful] at all, he was quite ugly. For this reason all the children school used to tease him and call him names. Sundarlal used to complai continually to his parents, 'Why was I given such a useless name. Is ther some shortage of good names in the world? Why wasn't I given som ordinary name like Ramlal or Krishna Kumar?' But who would listen t what he had to say. His father didn't even have the time to talk to him; h was busy running his shop all the time. And whenever Sundarlal began t say anything to his mother about his name she would say, 'Oh son do shu up, let me do my work, what do you know about these things'.

One day while reading the newspaper Sundarlal thought of something. sometimes so happens, doesn't it, he began to say to himself, that people' names are changed; it would be good if I too were to change my nam Taking the money from some friend he got a ticket for the Rajdha Express that goes to Delhi. He told his folks at home that he was going t his friend Rishi's birthday party and that he would be back in two days.

On the day when he was to go to Delhi he went secretly into the kitche and put himself some things to eat into a bag. The train was at half past te at night; but Sundarlal thought there would be such a crowd in the trai that latecomers wouldn't have a hope of getting a seat, so he left the hous at exactly nine. There was nobody in the house at that time, and even th streets seemed completely empty. Sundarlal didn't have much mone with him, so he decided that he shouldn't go to the station by bus, if h went on foot he'd save the (money of the) bus fare. When he arrived at th station he was very surprised to see that many seats in the train we (lying) empty. He got quite a good seat by the window; and as soon as h sat down on the berth he fell asleep.

'wo days later when he returned home he began wondering how he hould tell his parents that he had changed his name. Father would say You've dragged our family name through the mud', and Mother would ay who knows what.

t was morning time. Opening the door of his room he began listening arefully what was going on downstairs in the kitchen. His parents were alking about the wedding of some neighbour's son as they had their reakfast. When Sundarlal's mother shouted loudly 'Sundar, oh Sundar, ome, you'll get late', Sundarlal summoned up his courage and said, 'Ma, ny name isn't Sundar or Sundarlal. I've changed my name. Please call me Elvis" from now on.'

APPENDIX 4

Key to the exercises

1	*khag*	*cakh*	*jag*	*khaṭ*	*jhaṭ*		
	kac	*gaj*	*ṭak*	*ḍac*	*ḍag*		
	कण	ठन	जट	ठठ	कट		
	गण	जज	ढक	घट	ठग		
2	*tan*	*gaz*	*dhan*	*phaṭ*	*pad*		
	mat	*tab*	*man*	*jab*	*gat*		
	पढ़	मठ	ख़त	डफ	पब		
	नग	बम	कप	पथ	पट		
3	*dal*	*das*	*kam*	*ham*	*ghar*	*hal*	*man*
	taraf	*bacat*	*saṛak*	*naram*	*khabar*	*mahal*	*nagar*
	हद	पल	वट	सच	नल	हर	सब
	जड़	डर	भय	बस	शक	हक़	तय
	जगह	भजन	ग़जल	समय	मगर	लगन	क़लम
4	*ai*	*asar*	*os*	*ṛṇ*	*āh*		
	āg	*agar*	*ādar*	*aurat*	*ūn*		
	ऊपर	उमस	आ	ओ	आज		
	एकड़	ईद	अटल	और	अलग		
5	*gājar*	*salād*	*cāval*	*canā*	*pālak*		
	मसाला	शराब	पराठा	कबाब	मटर		
6	*mīṭar*	*binā*	*pītal*	*hisāb*	*dil*	*ṭhīk*	
	नामी	क़ीमत	कहानी	साड़ी	सिख	शिकायत	

7 *pul* *dhūl* *rūkhā* *sūd* *dūrī* *kabūtar*

सूखा रुको तू रूस तुम मुलायम

8 *keval* *khetī* *paise* *beṭā* *mez* *khairiyat*

बेकार पहेली मैला सिनेमा तेरा ठेकेदार

9 *dhokhā* *komal* *hauz* *dauṛo* *koṭhī*

बोलो जौ गोरा मौलिक करोड़

10 गए गई गाई गाओ जाएगा

धोओ धोइए धोए रुई रईस

रुलाई सोई बनाए बनाओ बढ़ई

11 *gẫv* *mahãgā* *ẫgan* *pũch* *dhuẫ* *ãdherā*

खाँसी सौंफ दोनों लौंग आईं मेज़ें

12 *sthiti* *svarūp* *sthāyī* *pistaul* *lasṭam-pasṭam*

स्वागत बस्ती स्लेट रास्ता स्नान स्मरण

13 *naqśā* *brāhmaṇ* *patthar* *koṣṭak* *kyõ* *niścay*

बिल्ली हिन्दू नाश्ता तुम्हारा अध्यापक अवश्य

पक्का ज़्यादा क़िस्मत हत्या नष्ट हल्दी

फ़ैक्टरी अक्सर लन्दन आत्मा गिरफ़्तार सत्य

14 छुट्टी बुद्ध मुहल्ला बच्चा अट्ठाईस गद्दा

चित्त विद्यार्थी द्वीप सह्य पद्म चिह्न

15	हिन्दी	मुम्बई	ठण्डा	अङ्ग	मनोरञ्जन
	मंडल	भंजन	लंबा	हिंदू	संघ
	बंदर	लंका	रंग	चिंता	घंटा

16	Chandigarh	Aurangabad	Indore	Ganga (Ganges)
	Madhya Pradesh	Bengal	Rajasthan	Pakistan
	Gwalior	Srinagar	Punjab	Gangotri

दिल्ली	यमुनोत्री	कलकत्ता	नाथद्वारा
उज्जैन	हरिद्वार	वृन्दाबन	दुर्गापुर
मुम्बई	महाराष्ट्र	भुबनेश्वर	अम्बाला
उत्तर	दक्षिण	पूर्व	पश्चिम
(north	south	east	west)

17 Tell me not in mournful numbers
life is but an empty dream;
For the soul is dead that slumbers
and things are not what they seem.

(The verse (by Longfellow) is quoted in Devanagari in the short story वारिस 'The heir' by the Hindi author Mohan Rakesh.)

18	Bharat (India)	Gujarat	Bihar	Dhaka	Allahabad
	Tamil Nadu	Lucknow	Karachi	Lahore	Dehra Dun
	Nepal	Mussoorie	Mathura	Kota	Varanasi
	Banaras	Yamuna	Himalaya	Kerala	Orissa

APPENDIX 5

The figures explained

The main text of all the illustrative figures that are not self-explanatory is transcribed and translated below.

Fig. 1. (a) यहाँ पर मच्छी व मुर्गे का ताजा मीट मिलता है

yahā̃ par macchī va murge kā tājā mīṭ miltā hai.

'Fresh fish and chicken meat is available here'.

(b) काजल आप्टीकल्स; यहाँ नजर के चश्मे जापानी मशीन द्वारा जाँच करके बनाये जाते ह

kājal āpṭīkals – yahā̃ najar ke caśme jāpānī maśīn dvārā jā̃c karke banāye jāte haĩ.

'Kajal Opticals – 'Here eye-glasses are made after [optical] testing with Japanese equipment'.

Fig. 4. इन्दू [इन्दु] आर्ट थियेटर एंड फिल्म सोसायटी (रजि.) की प्रस्तुति श्री गिरिश [गिरीश] कर्नाड लिखित नाटक तुग़लक...निर्देशक – यासीन खान. दिनांक – 26 फरवरी, समय 5.30 सांय [सायं], स्थान – एल. टी. जी. ऑडिटोरियम कॉपरनिक्स [कॉपरनिकस] मार्ग, मंडी हाउस, दिल्ली. टिकट – 100.50.25. टिकट उपलब्ध हैं – एल. टी. जी. आडिटोरियम काउन्टर, सम्पर्क सूत्र 2411107।

indū [indu] ārṭ thiyeṭar eṇḍ philm sosāyaṭī (raji.) kī prastuti śrī giriś [girīś] karnāḍ likhit nāṭak tuglak...nirdeśak – yāsīn khān. dinā̃k 26 pharvarī, samay 5.30 sā̃y [sāyaṃ], sthān – el. ṭī. jī. ā̃ḍiṭoriyam kā̃parniks [kā̃parnikas] mārg, maṇḍī hāus, dillī. ṭikaṭ – 100.50.25 ṭikaṭ uplabdh haĩ – el. ṭī. jī. āḍiṭoriyam kāunṭar, sampark sūtră 2411107.

'Presented by the Indu Art Theatre and Film Society (reg.), the play *Tuglak* written by Mr Girish Karnad. Director Yasin Khan. Date: 26 February, time 5.30 p.m., venue L.T.G. Auditorium, Copernicus Marg, Mandi House, Delhi. Tickets - [Rs.] 100, 50, 25. Tickets are available at L.T.G. Auditorium counter, contact 2411107.'

Fig. 6. Techno ENGINEERING *Works* स्पेश्लिस्ट शौकर रिफ़िलिंग All kind of SHOCKERS शौकर की गारन्टेड रिपेयर / सुपर ० चेतक ० एल एम एल ० मोपेड

Techno Engineering Works *speślisṭ śaukar rifiling* All kind of shockers *śaukar kī gāranṭeḍ ripeyar / supar - cetak - el em el - mopeḍ.*
'Techno Engineering Works specialist shocker refilling. All kinds of shockers / Super, Chetak, LML, moped.'

Fig 7. कुत्तों से सावधान

kuttõ se sāvdhān.

'Beware of dogs'.

Fig.8. श्री सीमेंट सॉलिड शक्ति

śrī sīmenṭ să̄liḍ śakti.

'Shri Cement: solid strength.'

Fig. 10. सीगड़ टेलर्स / लेडीज एण्ड जेन्ट्स / शे.ग्रा.बैंक के पास नवलगढ़ सर्वश्रेष्ठ सिलाई के लिए

sīgaṛ ṭelars / ledīj enḍ jenṭs / śe[khāvāṭī] grā[mīṇ] baink ke pās navalgaṛh sarvăśreṣṭh silāī ke lie.
'Sigar Tailors – Ladies and Gents – Near the Shekhavati Rural Bank, Navalgarh. For superior tailoring.'

Fig. 13. वीआईपी सुरक्षा / अतिविशिष्ट व्यक्तियों की व्यक्तिगत सुरक्षा के बारे में घोषित नई नीति स्वागत योग्य है। अनेक केंन्द्रीय गृहमंत्रियों ने सार्वजनिक रूप से यह स्वीकार किया है कि हमारी वीआईपी सुरक्षा व्यवस्था अनेक किस्म की परेशानियों का सबब बनती जा रही है। यह महसूस किया जा रहा था कि कुछ स्वार्थी लोग इस व्यवस्था को एक बड़े राजनैतिक रैकेट में तब्दील कर रहे थे। इसका एक नुकसान यह था कि सुरक्षा एजेंसियों का ध्यान अपने मूल कार्यों से हट जाता था और वे नेताओं तथा...

*vīāīpī surakṣā   ativiśiṣṭ vyaktiyõ kī vyaktigat surakṣā ke bāre mẽ
ghoṣit naī nīti svāgat yogyǎ hai. anek kendrīy gṛhmantriyõ ne
sārvajanik rūp se yah svīkār kiyā hai ki hamārī vīāīpī surakṣā
vyavasthā anek kism kī pareśāniyõ kā sabab bantā jā rahī hai. yah
mahsūs kiyā jā rahā thā ki kuch svārthī log is vyavasthā ko ek baṛe
rājnaitik raikeṭ mẽ tabdīl kar rahe the. iskā ek nuksān yah thā ki surakṣā
ejensiyõ kā dhyān apne mūl kāryõ se haṭ jātā thā aur ve netāõ tathā...*

'VIP Security. The new policy concerning the personal security of
VVIPs announced [recently] is to be welcomed. [NB: a *viśiṣṭ* person is
a VIP or 'very important person'; but as this designation has been
eroded by over-use, the new category of *ativiśiṣṭ* or VVIP 'very very
important person' has come into use.] Many central Home Ministers
have accepted publicly that our VVIP security system has been
becoming a matter for many kinds of concern. It was felt that some
selfish people were changing this system into a major political
'racket'. One harmful outcome of this was that the attention of security
agencies was diverted from their main functions and...

Fig. 16 (Lower part of text.). रु. 4000/- की महाबचत / जल्दी कीजिए
योजना सीमित समय तक उपलब्ध. अधिकृत विक्रेता / अमर ऑटोस /
६०३, कांती [कांति] नगर, स्वर्ण सिनेमा रोड, शाहदरा, दिल्ली. फोन...;

*ru. 4000/- kī mahābacat / jaldī kījie yojnā sīmit samay tak uplabdh /
adhikṛt vikretā / amar ǎṭos / 603, kāntī [kānti] nagar, svarṇ sinemā roḍ,
śāhdarā, dillī. phon:...*

'Mega-saving of Rs. 4000...Hurry, scheme available for a limited
period. Authorised dealer: Amar Motors, 603 Kanti Nagar, Svarna
Cinema Road, Shahdara, Delhi. Phone...'

Fig 18. ईम्पीरियल बारबर शॉप / लेडिज व जैन्ट्स ब्यूटी पार्लर हमारे यहाँ
ब्राइडल मेक-अप व ब्यूटिशियन कोर्स भी उपलब्ध है । *impiriyal bārbar
śǎp   leḍij va jainṭs byūṭī pārlar   hamāre yahǎ brāiḍal mek-ap va
byūṭīśiyan kors bhī uplabdh hai.*

'Imperial Barber Shop. Ladies' and Gents' Beauty Parlour. Bridal
make-up and beautician course also available here.

Fig. 21. शिव ट्रेडर्स...फो. 211134...कॉफी की मशीन बुक की जाती है. बर्थडे केक व बर्थडे का सभी सामान उचित रेट पर मिलता है.

śiv ṭredars...pho. 211134...kǎphī kī maśīn buk kī jātī hai. barthḍe kek va barthḍe kā sabhī sāmān ucit reṭ par miltā hai.

'Shiv Traders...phone 211134...Coffee machine is [available to be] booked. Birthday cakes and all birthday materials are available at reasonable rates.'

APPENDIX 6

Index of terms

akṣar – a character or syllable, especially of the Devanagari script.

alveolar – a sound produced by the front of the tongue in contact with the alveolar ridge, that part of the mouth just behind the upper teeth.

aspirate – a sound pronounced with audible breath.

conjunct – a Devanagari character comprising two consonants with no intervening vowel.

dental – a sound made by the tip and rim of the tongue against the teeth.

diphthong – a syllable containing two distinct and successive vowels, as in English 'mice', 'go', 'house', and in Hindi *gaī, gae.*

flap – an 'r' sound produced by rapid light contact between the tongue and the roof of the mouth.

fricative – a consonant sound produced by friction when the breath is forced through a restricted opening.

geminate – a doubled consonant.

halant – a consonant whose inherent vowel has been suppressed (as by the addition of *virām*).

inherent vowel – the vowel *a* as inherent part of an unmodified consonant, e.g. the *a* in म *ma.*

-kār – a suffix for naming letters, e.g. *ma-kār,* 'the character म', *i-kār,* 'the character इ'.

labial – a sound produced by the lips.

mātrā – a vowel sign written after a consonant.

neologism – a newly-coined word (in the Hindi context, usually one based on a Sanskrit root).

palatal – a sound pronounced by contact between the middle of the tongue and the hard palate.

retroflex – a sound produced when the tongue is curled back against the hard palate.

semi-vowel – a consonant which has some of the phonetic quality of a vowel: 'y', 'v'.

sibilant – a fricative hissing sound, such as 's', 'sh'.

sonant: see 'voicing'.

virām – the subscript sign ् which suppresses the inherent vowel.

velar – a sound produced by the back of the tongue in contact with the soft palate.

voicing – the production of a sound with the vibration of the vocal chords; 'b' is voiced, 'p' is voiceless. Voiced sounds are also called 'sonants', and unvoiced sounds 'surds'.

GLOSSARY

This glossary lists all the Hindi words that have been used in the main sections of the book, together with selected words from the illustrations. Personal names and English words are not generally included.

The dictionary order of Devanagari follows the syllabary matrix, which is repeated below for easy reference.

अ a	आ ā	इ i	ई ī	
उ u	ऊ ū	ऋ ṛ		
ए e	ऐ ai	ओ o	औ au	
क ka	ख kha	ग ga	घ gha	(ङ् ṅ)
च ca	छ cha	ज ja	झ jha	(ञ् ñ)
ट ṭa	ठ ṭha	ड ḍa	ढ ḍha	ण ṇa
त ta	थ tha	द da	ध dha	न na
प pa	फ pha	ब ba	भ bha	म ma
य ya	र ra	ल la	व va	
श śa	ष ṣa	स sa	ह ha	

The main points to bear in mind are:

- short vowels precede long vowels (e.g. मु *mu* precedes मू *mū)*
- unaspirated consonants precede aspirated consonants (e.g. क *ka* precedes ख *kha)*
- syllables with *candrabindu* or *anusvār* precede those without (e.g. हाँ *hā̃* precedes हा *hā,* and पंडित *paṇḍit* precedes पकना *paknā*)
- non-conjunct forms precede conjunct forms (e.g. टीन *ṭīn* precedes ट्रक *ṭrak*)
- dotted forms of consonants are not distinguished from their non-dotted equivalents in terms of sequence

अ *a*

अंग m *aṅg* limb

अंजन m *añjan* kohl, lampblack

अंडा m *aṇḍā* egg

अंदर *andar* inside

अँधेरा m *ā̃dherā* darkness

अंबाला m *ambālā* Ambala

अक्तूबर m *aktūbar* October

अक्षर m *akṣar* syllable, alphabet character

अक्सर *aksar* often, usually

अगर *agar* if

अगस्त m *agast* August

अग्रवाल m *agravāl* Agrawal (a merchant caste and surname)

अच्छा *acchā* good

अज्ञेय *ajñey* (pronounced *'agyey'*) unknowable

अटल *aṭal* immoveable, firm

अट्ठाईस *aṭṭhāīs* eighteen

अतः *ataḥ* therefore

अधिक *adhik* much, many, very, more

अध्यापक m *adhyāpak* teacher

अन्न m *ann* grain, food

अप्रैल m *aprail* April

अफ़ग़ानिस्तान m *afgānistān* Afghanistan

अफ़सर m *afsar* officer

अमर *amar* immortal, eternal

अम्मा f *ammā* mother

अलग *alag* separate, different, apart, aloof

अलमारी f *almārī* cupboard, almirah

अवश्य *avasyă* certainly

अविज्ञ *avijñă* ignorant, unaware

अष्ट *aṣṭ* eight, octo-

असर m *asar* effect, influence, impression

अस्पताल m *aspatāl* hospital

अस्सी *assī* eighty

आ *ā*

आँख f *ā̃kh* eye

आँगन m *ā̃gan* courtyard

आकाशवाणी f *ākāśvāṇī* 'heaven-voice', oracle; India's government radio network

आग[f] *āg* fire

आगरा[m] *āgrā* Agra

आज *āj* today

आज्ञा[f] *ājñā* command; order/permission to leave

आटा[m] *āṭā* flour

आठ *āṭh* eight

आत्मा[f] *ātmā* soul

आदमी[m] *ādmī* man; person

आदर[m] *ādar* respect, honour, esteem

आना *ānā* to come

आप *āp* you (formal); आपका *āpkā* your

आम[1 m] *ām* mango

आम[2] *ām* ordinary, common

आरंभ[m] *ārambh* commencement

आर्थिक *ārthik* financial

आर्द्र *ārdră* moist

आशा[f] *āśā* hope

आसान *āsān* easy

आह[f] *āh* sigh

आह्लाद[m] *āhlād* rapture

इ *i*

इँचाव[m] *ĩcāv* pulling, drawing

इँचीटेप[m] *ĩcīṭep* measuring tape

इंदौर *indaur* Indore

इंद्र *indră* Indra

इधर *idhar* here, over here; recently

इलाहाबाद m *ilāhābād* Allahabad

इश्क़ m *iśq* romantic love

इस्तरी f *istrī* clothes iron

ई *ī*

ईख f *īkh* sugarcane

ईद f *īd* Eid name of two Muslim festivals

ईमान m *īmān* honesty

उ *u*

उज्जैन m *ujjain* Ujjain

उड़ीसा m *uṛīsā* Orissa

उत्तर m, adj *uttar* north, northern

उत्तर प्रदेश m *uttar pradeś* Uttar Pradesh

उद्भव m *udbhav* origin, coming into being

उधर *udhar* there, over there

उन *un* them

उपलब्ध *uplabdh* available

उमदा, उम्दा *umdā* good

उमर, उम्र f *umar, umră* age

उमस f *umas* sultriness

ऊ *ū*

ऊँचा *ũcā* high, tall, great

ऊन[f] *ūn* wool

ऊपर *ūpar* up, above, upstairs

ऊब[m] *ūb* boredom, tedium

ऋ *ṛ*

ऋण[m] *ṛṇ* debt

ऋषि[m] *ṛṣi* sage

ऋषिकेश[m] *ṛṣikeś* Rishikesh

ए *e*

एअर इंडिया[m] *ear iṇḍiyā* Air India

एक *ek* one; a

एकड़[f] *ekaṛ* acre

एकाध *ekādh* one or two, a couple (of)

एक्स्प्रेस[f] *ekspres* express

एवं *evaṃ* and

ऐ *ai*

ऐ *ai* hey, oh

ऐक्ट्रेस[f] *aikṭres* actress

ऐनक[f] *ainak* spectacles

ऐश[m] *aiś* luxury, voluptuous enjoyment

ओ *o*

ओ *o* Oh

ओर[f] *or* direction

ओस[f] *os* dew

औ *au*

औरंगाबाद[m] *aurangābād* Aurangabad

और *aur* and; more

औरत[f] *aurat* woman

क *ka*, क़ *qa*

कंबल[m] *kambal* blanket

कई *kaī* several, many

कच[m] *kac* (archaic) hair

कटना *kaṭnā* to be cut

कण[m] *kaṇ* particle

कप[m] *kap* cup

कपड़ा[m] *kaprā* cloth; garment

कब *kab* when?

कबाब[m] *kabāb* kebab

कम *kam* little, less

कमल[m] *kamal* lotus

कमाल[m] *kamāl* miracle

करना *karnā* to do

कराची^f *karācī* Karachi

करोड़^m *karoṛ* crore, 100 lakhs, ten million

कर्तव्य^m *kartavyă* duty

कर्म^m *karmă* karma, action (especially as determining future births)

कल *kal* yesterday; tomorrow

कलकत्ता^m *kalkattā* Calcutta

क़लम^m/f *qalam* pen

कल्प^m *kalpă* aeon

कहाँ *kahā̃* where?

कहानी^f *kahānī* story

का, की, के *kā, kī, ke* possessive postposition (works like the English apostrophe 's' – राम की बेटी *rām kī beṭī* Ram's daughter)

काजल^m *kājal* kohl, lampblackकान^m *kān* ear

कॉपी^f *kâpī* copy book, exercise book

काफ़ी *kāfī* quite, very; enough, sufficient

काम^m *kām* work, task, matter in hand

कार^f *kār* car

-कार *-kār* suffix making a character name, e.g. ककार *kakār*, 'the character क *ka*'

कार्यक्रम^m *kāryakram* programme

काल^m *kāl* time, Time

काशी^f *kāśī* Varanasi, Banaras

कि *ki* that (conjunction)

किताब ^f *kitāb* book

क़िस्मत ^f *qismat* fate

क़ीमत ^f *qīmat* price, value

कील ^m *kīl* nail

कुआँ ^m *kuā̃* well

कुछ *kuch* some, somewhat

कुत्ता ^m *kuttā* dog

कुमार ^m *kumār* bachelor, prince

कुरसी ^f *kursī* chair

कुल ^m *kul* total, whole amount

कूल ^m *kūl* bank of river, pond

कृतज्ञ *kr̥tajñă* (pronounced '*kr̥tagyă*') grateful

कृपा ^f *kr̥pā* kindness, grace

कृषि ^f *kr̥ṣi* agriculture

कृष्ण ^m *kr̥ṣṇă* Krishna

के दौरान *ke daurān* during

के बावजूद *ke bāvăjūd* in spite of

के लिए *ke lie* for

केरल ^m *keral* Kerala

केला ^m *kelā* banana

केवल *keval* only

कोका-कोला ^m *kokā-kolā* Coca-Cola

कोटा ^m *koṭā* Kota

कोठी ^f *koṭhī* large house, bungalow, mansion

कोमल *komal* soft, delicate

कोर[f] *kor* (archaic) edge, tip

कोष्टक[m] *koṣṭak* bracket

कौन *kaun* who?कौर[m] *kaur* mouthful of food

क्या *kyā* what; (also converts a following statement into a question – यह राम है *yah rām hai* This is Ram > क्या यह राम है? *kyā yah rām hai?* Is this Ram?)

क्यों *kyõ* why

क्रम[m] *kram* sequence, order

क्रिकेट[m] *kriketฺ* cricket

क्षेत्र[m] *kṣetră* region, area, field

ख ***kha***, ख़ ***kha***

खग[m] *khag* (archaic) bird

खट, खट-खट[f] *khaṭ, khaṭ-khaṭ* knocking sound

खड़ा *khaṛā* standing, upright; खड़ी पाई[f] *khaṛī pāī* the sign '।' (= full stop); खड़ी बोली[f] *khaṛī bolī* the dialect on which Hindi and Urdu are based; the modern standard dialect of Hindi

ख़त[m] *khat* letter

ख़बर[f] *khabar* news, information

खाँसी[f] *khā̃sī* cough

खादी[f] *khādī* hand-spun cloth

खाना[1 m] *khānā* food

खाना[2] *khānā* to eat

ख़ाना^m *khānā* place of work (e.g. डाक-ख़ाना *ḍak-khānā* post office); square (on chessboard etc.)

खीझना *khījhnā* to be irritated; खीझ^f *khījh* irritation

खुलना *khulnā* to open, be opened

खेत^m *khet* field (agricultural)

खेती^f *khetī* farming

ख़ैरियत^m *khairiyat* well-being

खोलना *kholnā* to open

ख़ौफ़^m *khauf* fear, terror

खौलना *khaulnā* to boil

ख्याति^f *khyāti* fame

ग *ga*, ग़ *ga*

गंगा^f *gangā* the river Ganga, Ganges

गंगोत्री^f *gangotrī* Gangotri

गंद^m *gand* stench, filth

गंध^f *gandh* smell, fragrance, stench

गंभीर *gambhīr* serious; गंभीरता^f *gambhīrtā* seriousness

गज^m *gaj* (archaic) elephant

गज़^m *gaz* yard (measurement); bow of a musical instrument

ग़ज़ल^f *gazal* ghazal, a genre of poetry in Urdu and Hindi

गण^m *gaṇ* group

गत *gat* last, past, previous

गद्दा^m *gaddā* mattress

गरदन f *gardan* neck

गरम, गर्म *garam, garm* warm, hot

गाँव m *gā̃v* village

गाजर f *gājar* carrot

गाड़ी f *gāṛī* car; train

गाथा f *gāthā* ballad

गाना1 m *gānā* song

गाना2 *gānā* to sing

ग़ायब *g̱āyab* missing, absent

गार्ड m *gārḍ* guard

गिरफ़्तार *giraftār* arrested

गुजरात m *gujarāt* Gujarat

गुरु m *guru* guru, spiritual guide, teacher

गुसलख़ाना m *gusalk̲h̲ānā* bathroom

गोरा m, adj *gorā* fair-complexioned; a white person

ग्यारह *gyārah* eleven

ग्राम1 m *grām* villageग्राम2 m *grām* gram, gramme

ग्वालियर m *gvāliyar* Gwalior

घ *gha*

घट m *ghaṭ* pitcher, water-pot

घटना *ghaṭnā* to lessen, decrease

घर m *ghar* home, house

घाट^m *ghāṭ* riverbank, bathing steps

घात^f *ghāt* stratagem

घुसना *ghusnā* to enter, sneak in

घूस^f *ghūs* bribe

च *ca*

चंडीगढ़^m *caṇḍīgaṛh* Chandigarh

चख^m *cakh* (archaic) eye

चट^f, adv *caṭ* snapping; snappily

चना^m *canā* channa, chickpea

चमड़ी^f *camṛī* skin; hide

चलना *calnā* to move

चश्मा^m *caśmā* spectacles

चाँदिनी^f *cā̃dinī* moonlight

चॉकलेट^m *câkleṭ* chocolate

चाचा^m *cācā* uncle, father's younger brother

चाट^f *cāṭ* tasty snack

चार *cār* four

चावल^m *cāval* rice

चाहिए *cāhie* needed, wanted

चिट्ठी^f *ciṭṭhī* note, chit

चित्त^m *citt* mind

चिह्न^f *cihn* sign

चीनी^f *cīnī* sugar

चुड़ैल[f] *cuḍail* witch, ghost, hag

चुनना *cunnā* to choose

चुन्नी[f] *cunnī* woman's light scarf, wrap

चेचन्या[m] *cecnyā* Chechnya

चेत[m] *cet* consciousness, wits

चैत[m] *cait* name of a month (equivalent to March-April)

चोर[m] *cor* thief

चौंतीस *caũtīs* thirty-four

छ *cha*

छः *chaḥ* six

छनना *channā* to be sifted, strained

छलना[f] *chalnā* deceipt, illusion

छह *chah* six

छुट्टी[f] *chuṭṭī* holiday

छोड़ना *choṛnā* to leave, abandon

छोर[m] *chor* edge, border

ज *ja*, ज़ *za*

जग[m] *jag* world

जगह[f] *jagah* place

जज[m] *jaj* judge

जट[m] *jaṭ* Jat (a caste)

जड़[f] *jaṛ* root, basis, origin

जनता[f] *janătā, jantā* people, the public

जनवरी[f] *janvarī* January

जन्म[m] *janmă, janam* birth

जब *jab* when

जल[m] *jal* water

जल्दी *jaldī* quickly

जाँच[f] *jā̃c* test, examination, inspection

जाति[f] *jāti* caste

जानना *jānā* to know

जानवर[m] *jānvar* animal

जाना *jānā* to go; (also forms passive with participle of main verb; active लिखना *likhnā* to write > passive लिखा जाना *likhā jānā* to be written)जाने *jāne* who knows, heaven knows

जापानी *jāpānī* Japanese

जी नहीं *jī nahī̃* no

जी हाँ *jī hā̃* yes

जीवन[m] *jīvan* life

जुलाई[f] *julāī* July

जूठा *jūṭhā* despoiled by touch (e.g. food touched by someone else)

जून[m] *jūn* June

जैन[m] *jain* Jain

जैसलमेर[m] *jaisalmer* Jaisalmer

जो *jo* the one who

जौ m *jau* barley

ज्ञान m *jñān* (pronounced '*gyān*') knowledge

ज़्यादा *zyādā* more

ज्योत्स्ना f *jyotsnā* (archaic) moonlight

ज्वाला f *jvālā* blaze, flame, burning

झ *jha*

झट *jhaṭ* instantly

झूठ m, adj *jhūṭh* lie, falsehood; false

झूठा *jhūṭhā* false, lying, insincere

ट *ṭa*

टक f *ṭak* (archaic) stare, gaze

टाल f *ṭāl* postponing, putting off

टीका m *ṭīkā* forehead-mark

टीन m *ṭīn* tin, can

टी-वी f *ṭī-vī* TV, television

टेलर m *ṭelar* tailor

ट्रक f *ṭrak* truck

ट्रेन f *ṭren* train

ठ *ṭha*

ठंडा *ṭhaṇḍā* cold

ठग m *ṭhag* bandit, ritual murderer

ठठ, ठट्ठ^m *ṭhaṭh, ṭhaṭṭh* (archaic) crowd, throng

ठन^f *ṭhan* clanging sound

ठीक *ṭhīk* all right, OK, good

ठीका, ठेका^m *ṭhīkā, ṭhekā* contract

ठेकेदार^m *ṭhekedār* contractor

ड *ḍa*

डग^f *ḍag* step, pace, stride

डच *ḍac* Dutch

डफ^m *ḍaph* a tambourine-like drum

डर^m *ḍar* fear, dread

डाक्टर^m *ḍākṭar* doctor

डाल^f *ḍāl* branch (of tree)

डिब्बा^m *ḍibbā* box, compartment

डीज़ल^m *ḍīzal* diesel oil

डेथ^f *ḍeth* death

डोल^m *ḍol* rocking, swinging; swing

डौल^m *ḍaul* shape, form, appearance, style

ड्योढ़ी^f *ḍyoṛhī* porch, threshold

ड्राइंग^f *ḍrāiṅg* drawing

ड्राइवर^m *ḍrāivar* driver

ढ *ḍha*

ढकना *ḍhaknā* to cover, to be covered

ढाई *ḍhāī* two and a half

ढाका[m] *ḍhākā* Dhaka

ढाबा[m] *ḍhābā* eating place, cafe

ढाल[f] *ḍhāl* incline, slope

त *ta*

तक *tak* until, up to

तत्सम[m, adj] *tatsam* 'same as that' – describing a Sanskrit loanword that has retained its original form

तद्भव[m, adj] *tadbhav* 'of the nature of that' – describing a word deriving from Sanskrit but organically changed over time

तन[m] *tan* body

तब *tab* then

तबला[m] *tablā* tabla drum

तमिल नाडु[m] *tamil nāḍu* Tamil Nadu

तय *tay* decided, settled

तरकीब[f] *tarkīb* means, plan, contrivance

तरफ़[f] *taraf* direction, side

तरह[f] *tarah* way, manner

तस्वीर[f] *tasvīr* picture

ताऊ[m] *tāū* uncle (father's elder brother)

ताज[m] *tāj* crown, diadem

ताज महल[m] *tāj mahal* Taj Mahal

ताज़ा *tāzā* fresh

ताना[m] *tānā* taunt, jibe

ताल^m *tāl* musical time, rhythmic cycle of a fixed number of beats

ताला^m *tālā* lock

ताली^f *tālī* hand-clapping, beat

तीन *tīn* three

तुम *tum* you (familiar)

तुम्हारा *tumhārā* (relates to तुम *tum*)

तू *tū* you (intimate)

तृण^m *tṛṇ* blade of grass or straw

तेईस *teīs* twenty-three

तेरा *terā* your (relates to तू *tū*)

थ *tha*

थकना *thaknā* to become tired

थाना^m *thānā* police station

थाली^f *thālī* platter, tray

थैला^m *thailā* soft bag

द *da*

दंड^m *daṇḍ* staff, stick; punishment; the sign '।' (full stop)

दक्षिण^m, adj *dakṣiṇ* south, southern

दम^m *dam* breath, life

दर्पण^m *darpaṇ* mirror (especially in metaphorical senses)

दस *das* ten

दरिद्र *daridră* poor, indigent

दर्शन m *darśan* vision, sight; audience or meeting with esteemed person

दल m *dal* party, group, faction

दस *das* ten

दाँत m *dā̃t* tooth

दादा m *dādā* grandfather (father's father); gangster, 'godfather'

दादी f *dādī* grandmother (father's mother)

दाम m *dām* price

दाल f *dāl* lentil, split-pea

दास m *dās* slave

दिन m *din* day

दिल m *dil* heart

दिल्ली f *dillī* Delhi

दिसंबर m *disambar* December

दीन 1 m *dīn* religion

दीन 2 *dīn* wretched, poor

दीवाली f *dīvālī* Diwali, festival of light

दीया, दिया m *dīyā, diyā* oil lamp

दु:ख m *duḥkh* sorrow, suffering, unhappiness

दुर्गापुर m *durgāpur* Durgapur

दूतावास m *dūtāvās* embassy

दूध m *dūdh* milk

दूर *dūr* far, distant

दूरदर्शन m *dūrdarśan* television; India's government TV network

दूसरा *dūsrā* second, other

देव m *dev* god

देवनागरी f *devnāgarī* the Devanagari script

देवीकोट m *devīkoṭ* Devikot

देश m *deś* country, region

देहरा दून m *dehrā dūn* Dehra Dun

दो *do* two

दैव *daiv* divine

दौड़ना *dauṛnā* to run

दौलत f *daulat* wealth, riches

द्वारा *dvārā* by means (of), with

द्विज m *dvij* twice-born, Brahmin

द्वीप m *dvīp* island

ध *dha*

धन m *dhan* wealth

धन्यवाद *dhanyavād* thank you

धर्म m *dharm* religion, religious or moral duty

धर्मेतर *dharmetar* secular

धीरे *dhīre* slowly

धुआँ m *dhuā̃* smoke

धुलना *dhulnā* to be washed

धूप f *dhūp* sunshine

धूल f *dhūl* dust

धोखा m *dhokhā* trick, deceipt

धोना *dhonā* to wash

ध्यान m *dhyān* attention, concentration

न *na*

नक़्शा m *naqśā* map, plan, chart

नग m *nag* gem

नगर m *nagar* city, town

नज़र f *nazar* eye; glance

नदी f *nadī* river

नमक m *namak* salt

नमस्ते f *namaste* 'I salute you' – said for 'hello' and 'goodbye' (often with hands folded)

नया (नई/नयी, नए/नये) *nayā (naī/nayī, nae/naye)* new

नरम *naram* soft, mild

नल m *nal* tap, pipe

नव *nav* new

नवंबर m *navambar* November

नष्ट *naṣṭ* destroyed, ruined

नहर f *nahar* canal

नहीं *nahī̃* no; not

नाई m *naī* barber

नाक f *nāk* nose

नाथद्वारा m *nāthdvārā* Nathdwara

नान f *nān* naan, a flat bread cooked in *tandūr* (clay oven)

नानी f *nānī* grandmother (mother's father)

नापसंद *nāpasand* disliked

नाम^{m} *nām* name; नामी *nāmī* famous, renowned

नाश्ता^{m} *nāśtā* breakfast, light meal

निश्चय^{m} *niścay* certainty, resolve, decision

नीला *nīlā* blue

नेपाल^{m} *nepāl* Nepal

नौ *nau* nine

नौकर^{m} *naukar* servant

प *pa*

पंजाबी *pañjābī* Punjabi

पंडित^{m} *paṇḍit* pandit, Brahmin, scholar

पकना *paknā* to ripen, be cooked

पक्का *pakkā* firm, definite, solid-built, thoroughgoing

पट^{m} *paṭ* board, flat surface, name-plate

पड़ोसी^{m} *paṛosī* neighbour

पढ़ना *paṛhnā* to read, study

पता^{m} *patā* address, whereabouts; information, knowledge

पत्ता^{m} *pattā* leaf

पत्थर^{m} *patthar* stone

पथ^{m} *path* path, way

पद^{m} *pad* position, job

पद्म^{m} *padmă* lotus

पन्ना^{m} *pannā* page

पब *pab* pub

पर[1] *par* on; at

पर[2] *par* but

परदा, पर्दा[m] *pardā* curtain, purdah

पराठा[m] *parāṭhā* paratha, flaky layered flat-bread cooked in ghee on griddle

परिश्रम[m] *pariśram* hard work, effort

पल[m] *pal* moment

पश्चिम[m, adj] *paścim* west, western

पहुँचना *pahũcnā* to reach, arrive; पहुँच[f] *pahũc* reach

पहेली[f] *pahelī* riddle

पाँच *pā̃c* five

पाकिस्तान[m] *pākistān* Pakistan

पाट[m] *pāṭ* board, flat surface, flat stone

पाठ[m] *pāṭh* chapter of book; recitation of text

पानी[m] *pānī* water

पार *pār* across

पालक[m] *pālak* spinach

पिटना *piṭnā* to be beaten

पिता[m] *pitā* father

पीटना *pīṭnā* to beat

पीतल[m] *pītal* brass

पुत्र[m] *putră* son

पुरा[m] *purā* quarter of town

पुराना *purānā* old

पुरुष m *puruṣ* man, male, human being

पुल m *pul* bridge

पुलिस f *pulis* police

पूँछ f *pū̃ch* tail

पूछना *pūchnā* to ask

पूरा *pūrā* complete, full

पूर्व m, adj *pūrvă* east, eastern

पेट m *peṭ* stomach

पैदा *paidā* born, produced

पैसा, पैसे m *paisā, paise* money

पौधा m *paudhā* plant

प्रायः *prāyaḥ* generally

प्रेम m *prem* love

फ *pha*, फ़ *fa*

फट *phaṭ* at once

फ़रवरी f *farvarī* February

फ़र्ज़ m *farz* duty, obligation

फल m *phal* fruit

फिर *phir* then; again

फ़िल्म f *film* film, movie

फ़ुट m *fuṭ* foot

फूट[f] *phūṭ* bursting, break

फूल[m] *phūl* flower

फेल *phel* fail, failed

फ़ैक्टरी[f] *faikṭarī* factory

फैलना *phailnā* to spread

फ़्लू[m] *flū* flu

ब *ba*

बंगाल[m] *bangāl* Bengal

बंद *band* closed

बंध[m] *bandh* embankment, bund

बचत[f] *bacat* saving, savings, economy

बचना *bacnā* to be saved, to escape, survive

बच्चा[m] *baccā* child

बटना, बँटना *baṭnā, bãṭnā* to be divided; बटे *baṭe* divided by, over

बट्टा[m] *baṭṭā* rebate

बड़ा *baṛā* big

बढ़ई[m] *baṛhaī* carpenter

बढ़ाना *baṛhānā* to increase, advance

बत्ती[f] *battī* light, lamp

बदलना *badalnā* to change; to be changed

बनाना *banānā* to make

बनारस[m] *banāras* Banaras (Benares), Varanasi

बम[m] *bam* bomb

बरस[m] *baras* year

बल[m] *bal* force, strength

बला[m] *balā* calamity

बल्ला[m] *ballā* beam, pole

बस[m] *bas* control, power

बस्ती[f] *bastī* inhabitation, especially of huts in slum area

बहु[f] *bahu* daughter-in-law

बहुत *bahut* much, many, very

बाँस[m] *bā̃s* bamboo, bamboo pole

बाईस *bāīs* twenty-two

बाज़ार[m] *bāzār* market

बाड़[f] *bāṛ* fence, enclosure

बाढ़[f] *bāṛh* flood

बाद *bād* later, afterwards

बादल[m] *bādal* cloud

बाल[m] *bāl* hair

बॉल[m] *bâl* ball

बास[m] *bās* fragrance

बाहर *bāhar* out, outside, away

बिजली[f] *bijlī* electricity; lightning

बिना *binā* without

बिल्ली[f] *billī* cat

बिहार[m] *bihār* Bihar

बीस *bīs* twenty

बुद्ध[m] *buddhă* Buddha

बुरा *burā* bad

बुलाना *bulānā* to call

बेकार *bekār* useless; unemployed

बेटा[m] *beṭā* son, child

बेटी[f] *beṭī* daughter

बेल[m] *bel* wood-apple

बैठा *baiṭhā* seated, sitting

बैल[m] *bail* bullock

बोतल[f] *botal* bottle

बोर *bor* bore, bored

बोलना *bolnā* to speak

बोली[f] *bolī* speech, dialect

बौर[m] *baur* mango blossom

ब्राह्मण[m] *brāhmaṇ* Brahmin

भ *bha*

भंजन[m] *bhañjan* breaking

भंडार[m] *bhaṇḍār* store, shop

भगवद्गीता[f] *Bhagavadgītā* ('song of the Lord' – Sanskrit religious text)

भजन[m] *bhajan* hymn

भद्दा *bhaddā* clumsy, awkward

भय[m] *bhay* fear, misgivings

भरत[m] *bharat* Bharat, Rama's brother (in the Ramayana epic)

भाई m *bhāī* brother

भारत m *bhārat* India

भाषा f *bhāṣā* language

भिड़ f *bhiṛ* hornet

भी *bhī* also; even

भीड़ f *bhīṛ* crowd

भुबनेश्वर m *bhubaneśvar* Bhubaneshwar

भूकंप m *bhūkamp* earthquake

भू-खंड m *bhū-khaṇḍ* region of the earth

भूख f *bhūkh* hunger

भूमि f *bhūmi* earth, ground

भैया m *bhaiyā* brother, friend

भ्रष्ट *bhraṣṭ* corrupt

म *ma*

मंडल m *maṇḍal* circle

मई f *maī* May

मकान m *makān* house

मगर *magar* but

मच्छी f *macchī* fish

मटर m *maṭar* pea

मठ m *maṭh* monastery

मत m *mat* opinion, thought, creed

मथुरा m *mathurā* Mathura

मधुरता[f] *madhurtā* sweetness

मध्य प्रदेश[m] *madhyă pradeś* Madhya Pradesh

मन[m] *man* mind, heart

मनोरंजन[m] *manorañjan* entertainment

मशीन[f] *maśīn* machine, equipment

मसलन *maslan* for example

मसाला[m] *masālā* spice, ingredients, materials

मसूरी[f] *masūrī* Mussoorie

महँगा *mahãgā* expensive

महल[m] *mahal* palace

महाराष्ट्र[m] *mahārāṣṭră* Maharashtra

महावर[m] *mahāvar* lac (a red dye used by married women to decorate the soles of their feet)

महिला[f] *mahilā* lady, woman

माँ[f] *mā̃* mother, mum

मात्रा[f] *mātrā* vowel sign

मान[m] *mān* pride, honour, reputation

मार्च[m] *mārc* March

मित्र[m, f] *mitră* friend

मिल[f] *mil* mill

मिलना *milnā* to meet , be available

मिस्तरी[m] *mistrī* skilled artisan, mechanic, mason

मीट[m] *mīṭ* meat

मीटर[m] *mīṭar* metre

मीटिंग[f] *mīṭiṅg* meeting

मीठा *mīṭhā* sweet

मीनार^f *mīnar* tower, minaret

मील^m *mīl* mile

मुंबई^f *mumbaī* Mumbai, Bombay

मुग़ल^m, adj *mugal* Mughal

मुर्ग़ा, मुर्ग़^m *murg, murgā* fowl, chicken (fem मुर्ग़ी^f *murgī*)

मुहल्ला^m *muhallā* district of town, quarter

मृग^m *mṛg* deer

मृत्यु^f *mṛtyu* death

में *mẽ* in

मेज़^f *mez* table

मेला^m *melā* fair (festival)

मेहनत^f *mehnat* hard work, labour

मैं *maĩ* I

मैला *mailā* dirty

मोटा *moṭā* fat, stout, course

मोड़ना *moṛnā* to turn

मोढ़ा^m *moṛhā* bamboo stool

मोर^m *mor* peacock

मौत^f *maut* death

मौलिक *maulik* original

मौसा^m *mausā* uncle (husband of mother's sister)

मौसी^f *mausī* aunt (mother's sister)

य *ya*

यमुना[f] *yamunā* the river Yamuna, Jumna

यमुनोत्री[f] *yamunotrī* Yamunotri

यह *yah* this, he, she, it

यहाँ *yahā̃* here; यहाँ पर *yahā̃ par* here, at this place

ये *ye* these, they

योजना[f] *yojnā* plan, scheme

र *ra*

रंग[m] *raṅg* colour

रईस[m] *raīs* aristocrat

रज़ाई[f] *razāī* cotton-filled quilt

रसोईघर[m] *rasoīghar* kitchen

राजधानी[f] *rājdhānī* capital city

राजस्थान[m] *rājasthān* Rajasthan

राजा[m] *rājā* king

राम[m] *rām* Ram, Rama

राष्ट्र[m] *rāṣṭră* nation

रास्ता, रस्ता[m] *rāstā, rastā* road

रुई, रूई[f] *ruī, rūī* cotton

रुपया[m] *rupayā* rupee

रुलाई[f] *rulāī* crying, weeping

रूप[m] *rūp* form, beauty

रेखा[f] *rekhā* line

रेडियो m *reḍiyo* radio

रोशनी f *rośnī* light, brightness

ल *la*

लंबा *lambā* tall, high

लखनऊ m *lakhnaū* Lucknow

लगन f *lagan* love, attachment

लड़का m *laṛkā* boy

लड़की f *laṛkī* girl

लस्टम-पस्टम *lasṭam-pasṭam* somehow or other, any old how

लाजवाब *lajavāb* without equal

लाल *lāl* red

लाहौर m *lāhaur* Lahore

लिपि f *lipi* script, alphabet

लूट f *lūṭ* loot, looting, plunder

लोग m pl *log* people

लोटना *loṭnā* to roll, sprawl

लौंग f *laũg* clove

लौटना *lauṭnā* to return

व *va*

व *va* and

वट m *vaṭ* banyan tree

वर्ण m *varṇă* syllable ; वर्ण-माला f *varṇă-mālā* syllabary, alphabet

वह *vah* (often pronounced *vo*) that, he, she, it

वाराणसी^f *vārāṇasī* Varanasi, Banaras

विकसित *vikăsit* developed

विक्रेता^m *vikretā* seller, distributor

विद्या^f *vidyā* knowledge, learning

विद्यार्थी^m *vidyārthī* student

विशेषज्ञ^m *viśeṣajñă* (pronounced '*viśeṣagyă*') specialist

वीआईपी^m (वी० आई० पी०) *vīāīpī (vī. āī. pī.)* V.I.P.

वृंदाबन^m *vṛndāban* Vrindaban

वे *ve* those, they

व्यस्त *vyast* busy

श *śa*

शक^m *śak* doubt, suspicion

शक्ति^f *śakti* power, strength

शराब^f *śarāb* alcoholic drink

शर्म^f *śarm* shame, shyness, bashfulness

शर्मा^m *śarmā* Sharma (a Brahmin surname)

शिकायत^f *śikāyat* complaint

शुद्ध *śuddh* pure

शुरू^m *śurū* beginning

शूटिंग^f *śūṭing* shooting (of film)

शून्य^m, adj *śūnyă* zero, void

शैली^f *śailī* style

शोर^m *śor* noise, racket

शौकर^m *śaukar* 'shocker', vehicle's shock-absorber

श्रम m *śram* toil, exertion

श्री *śrī* Mr; Lord (e.g. श्री राम *śrī rām* Lord Rama)

श्रीनगर m *śrīnagar* Shrinagar

श्री लंका m *śrī lankā* Sri Lanka

स *sa*

संगीत m *sangīt* music

संघ m *sangh* association

संवत m *samvat* era; the 'Vikram samvat' calendrical era, starting 56/57 years BC (so that e.g. 2000 AD = 2056/57 V.S.)

संस्कृत f *sanskṛt* Sanskrit

संस्कृति f *sanskṛti* culture

सच m, adj *sac* true; truth

सटना *saṭnā* to be stuck, joined

सट्टा m *saṭṭā* transaction

सड़क f *saṛak* road, street

सताना *satānā* to torment

सत्ता f *sattā* power, authority

सत्य m *satyă* truth

सन m *san* hemp, cannabis

सन्न *sann* numbed

सप्ताह m *saptāh* week

सब *sab* all

सब्ज़ी m *sabzī* vegetable

सभ्य *sabhya* civilised

समझना *samajhnā* to understand; समझ[f] *samajh* understanding

समय[m] *samay* time

समस्या[f] *samasyā* problem

समान *samān* equal

सम्मान[m] *sammān* respect

सरकना *saraknā* to slip, creep

सरकार[f] *sarkār* government

सर्वश्रेष्ठ *sarvăśreṣṭh* best of all, superlative

सलाद *salād* salad

सस्ता *sastā* cheap, inexpensive

सह्य *sahyă* bearable

साक्षर *sākṣar* literate; साक्षरता[f] *sākṣartā* literacy

साग[m] *sāg* greens, green vegetables, e.g. spinach

साड़ी[f] *sāṛī* sari

सात *sāt* seven

साथ[m, adj] *sāth* company, with, along with

साफ़ *sāf* clean

सामान[m] *sāmān* goods, luggage, furniture

सारा *sārā* whole, entire

सावधान *sāvdhān* cautious, aware

सिंघाड़ा[m] *sĩghāṛā* water chestnut

सिंधु[f] *sindhu* the river Sindhu, Indus

सिंह[m] *sĩh* (often pronounced '*sing*') lion

सिख[m, adj] *sikh* Sikh

सितंबर m *sitambar* September

सितार m *sitār* sitar

सिनेमा m *sinemā* cinema

सिर m *sir* head

सिल m *sil* stone, grinding stone, flagstone

सिलाई f *silāī* sewing, stitching

सीख m *sīkh* instruction, teaching, moral advice

सीख़ f *sī<u>kh</u>* skewer

सीटी f *sīṭī* whistle

सीमित *sīmit* limited, restricted

सील f *sīl* dampness

सुंदर *sundar* beautiful, handsome, fine; सुंदरता f *sundartā* beauty

सुख m *sukh* happiness, pleasure

सुनना *sunnā* to hear , listen

सुरक्षा f *surakṣā* security, safety

सूअर m *sūar* pig

सूखना *sūkhnā* to dry

सूखा *sūkhā* dry

सूना *sūnā* deserted, empty

से *se* with, from, by

सेब m *seb* apple

सेर m *ser* a weight of about 1 kilogram

सेवा f *sevā* service

सैर f *sair* excursion

सो *so* so

सोना[1 m] *sonā* gold

सोना[2] *sonā* to sleep

सौंफ[f] *saũph* fennel

सौ *sau* hundred

स्कूल[m] *skūl* school

स्टेशन[m] *sṭeśan* station

स्त्री[f] *strī* woman

स्थान[m] *sthān* place

स्थायी *sthāyī* permanent, enduring, stable

स्थिति[f] *sthiti* situation

स्नान[m] *snān* bathing

स्पष्ट *spaṣṭ* clear, evident, distinct

स्मरण[m] *smaraṇ* recollection

स्मृति[f] *smṛti* memory

स्याही[f] *syāhī* ink

स्लेट[m] *sleṭ* slate, writing slate

स्वर[m] *svar* note, tone

स्वरूप[m] *svarūp* shape, form, character

स्वर्गीय *svargīyă* the late, deceased (lit.'heavenly')

स्वागत[m] *svāgat* welcome

ह *ha*

हंस[m] *hans* goose, swan

हँसना *hãsnā* to laugh

हँसी^f *hãsī* laughter

हक़^m *haq* right, privilege

हत्या^f *hatyā* murder

हद^f *had* limit, boundary, extent

हम *ham* we, us

हमारा *hamārā* our, ours; हमारे यहाँ *hamāre yahā̃* at our place

हर *har* each, every

हरिद्वार^m *haridvār* Haridwar

हल^1m *hal* plough

हल^2.m *hal* solution, resolution

हल्दी^f *haldī* turmeric

हाँ *hā̃* yes

हा *hā* ah!

हाथ^m *hāth* hand

हिंदी^f *hindī* Hindi

हिंदुस्तान^m *hindustān* India; northern India

हिंदू^m *hindū* Hindu

हिमाचल प्रदेश^m *himācal prades̒* Himachal Pradesh

हिमालय^m *himālay* Himalaya(s)

हिसाब^m *hisāb* account, calculation

हूँ *hū̃* am

हे *he* Oh! hey!

हैं *haĩ* are

है *hai* is

होंठ m *hõṭh* lip

होटल m *hoṭal* hotel, cafe, restaurant

होशियार *hośiyār* clever, intelligent

हौज़ m *hauz* tank, reservoir

हौले *haule* softly, gently

ह्रस्व *hrasvă* short (of vowel etc.)

Some further reading

Barz, Richard and Yogendra Yadav, 1991: *An Introduction to Hindi and Urdu.* 4th edn. Canberra: Australian National University. [Includes a detailed section on handwriting.]

Bhatia, Tej. K., 1996: *Colloquial Hindi.* London: Routledge. [With handwriting practice.]

Bright, William, 1996: 'The Devanagari Script', in Peter T. Daniels and William Bright (eds), *The World's Writing Systems.* New York and Oxford: Oxford University Press. pp. 384–390. [A clear statement on the development of the script.]

Coulson, Michael, 1976: *Sanskrit: an Introduction to the Classical Language.* London: Hodder & Stoughton. [Gives a very clear account of Devanagari, and advice for the left-handed.]

Kendrīya Hindī Nideśālay, 1989: देवनागरी लिपि तथा हिन्दी वर्तनी का मानकीकरण *Devanāgari lipi tathā hindī vartanī kā mānakīkaraṇ.* Delhi: Education Department, Govt. of India. [The official line on script conventions, not all of which find favour in the present manual. Hindi medium.]

Kesavan, B.S., 1997: *Origins of Printing and Publishing in the Hindi Heartland* (Vol. III of *History of Printing and Publishing in India: a Story of Cultural Re-awakening.* Delhi: National Book Trust. [Includes much cultural information.]

Lambert, H.M., 1953: *Introduction to the Devanagari Script for Students of Sanskrit and Hindi.* London: Oxford University Press. [With examples in fine handwritten Devanagari, and transliterations in IPA.]

Lexus, *Hindi & Urdu: a Rough Guide Phrasebook.* London, Rough Guides, 1997. [Excellent phrasebook in a portable format.]

Masica, Colin P., 1991: *The Indo-Aryan Languages.* Cambridge: Cambridge University Press. [Chapter 6, 'Writing Systems', gives a detailed history of Devanagari and related scripts.]

McGregor, R.S., 1993: *The Oxford Hindi-English Dictionary.* Oxford: Oxford University Press. [Includes Roman transliterations of each Nagari headword; an essential source for etymologies.]

McGregor, R.S., 1995: *Outline of Hindi Grammar.* 3rd edn. Oxford: Oxford University Press. [Includes a detailed discussion of the phonetics and pronunciation of Hindi; and, in the 3rd edition only, a section on handwriting.]

Robinson, Francis (ed.), 1989: *The Cambridge Encyclopedia of India, Pakistan, Bangladesh, Sri Lanka, Nepal, Bhutan and the Maldives.* Cambridge: Cambridge University Press. [pp. 406-409 article on 'Scripts' gives a comparative perspective.]

Salomon, Richard G., 1996: 'Brahmi and Kharoshthi', in Peter T. Daniels and William Bright (eds), *The World's Writing Systems.* New York and Oxford: Oxford University Press. pp. 373–383. [On the precursor of Devanagari.]

Shackle, Christopher, 1994: 'Scripts, Indian, Northern', in R.E. Asher (ed.), *The Encyclopedia of Language and Linguistics*, Oxford, Pergamon Press, Vol. 7, pp. 3697-3702. [A very lucid overview.]

Shackle, Christopher, and Rupert Snell, 1990: *Hindi and Urdu since 1800: a Common Reader.* London: School of Oriental and African Studies. [Includes analysis of Hindi phonetics and script.]

Shapiro, Michael C., 1989: *A Primer of Modern Standard Hindi.* Delhi: Motilal Banarsidass. [Includes a full introduction to the script.]

Snell, Rupert, with Simon Weightman, 2000: *Teach Yourself Hindi.* Revised edn. London: Hodder & Stoughton. [Complements this book with a full introduction to the Hindi language.]

THIS BOOK IS

Janet

. . . .

THE WORLD'S MOST TE/ RUDE/
GLAMOROUS/ HORRID/ SEXY/ UGLY/
LOVABLE/ BORING/ SAGITTARIAN

YOURS IN DISGUST/ KIND REGARDS/
ALL MY LOVE . . . Julie ☺ . . . .

P.S. PLEASE TAKE NOTE OF PAGE(S)

. . . .

THE SAGITTARIUS BOOK

A CORGI BOOK 0 552 12324 2

First publication in Great Britain
PRINTING HISTORY
Corgi edition published 1983
Corgi edition reissued 1984

Corgi Books are published by Transworld Publishers Ltd.,
Century House, 61-63 Uxbridge Road, Ealing, London W5 5SA.

Made and printed in Great Britain by the
Guernsey Press Co. Ltd., Guernsey, Channel Islands.

THE SAGITTARIUS BOOK

BY
IAN HEATH

SAGITTARIUS

NOVEMBER 23 - DECEMBER 20

NINTH SIGN OF THE ZODIAC

SYMBOL : THE ARCHER
RULING PLANET : JUPITER
COLOURS : PURPLE, WINE
GEM : ZIRCON
NUMBER : THREE
DAY : THURSDAY
METAL : TIN
FLOWER : CARNATION

ZZZZZZZZZ
The SAGITTARIAN at work................

..........IS FLEXIBLE..............

....HAS TO BE ORGANISED ....

........RULES BY THE CLOCK ....

...HAS TO WIN ARGUMENTS........

.... IS A QUICK THINKER............

...GETS ON WELL WITH COLLEAGUES....

......CAN BE TACTLESS..................

...........IS CLUMSY...................

....MAKES SILLY MISTAKES.........

....AND LOOKS-UP TO OTHERS.

The
SAGITTARIAN
finds success as...

......A DEBT COLLECTOR...........

........REMOVAL MAN....................

........DOG-BREEDER...............

COFFEE-TASTER

NURSE

GLASSCUTTER

...OR ADVERTISING EXECUTIVE.

ZZZZZZZZ
The SAGITTARIAN at home........

......ENJOYS LOUD MUSIC..........

........KEEPS CHICKENS..............

........EATS A LOT.....................

..WATCHES NATURE FILMS ON T.V.....

.....LOATHES IRONING..................

....KEEPS THE CAR CLEAN..............

......THE HOUSE SPOTLESS..........

.....ENJOYS WALLPAPERING.......

PLAYS CARDS

...AND IS A GOOD NEIGHBOUR.

The SAGITTARIAN likes.................

FISH SOUP

WINDSURFING

......BEING NOTICED..............

....COOKING EXOTIC DISHES......

SOLITUDE

.....AND EATING OUT.

The SAGITTARIAN dislikes........

. . . . LUMPY CUSTARD . . . .

RUDE WAITERS

...PAYING FOR CARRIER-BAGS.......

......PEOPLE WHO GOSSIP..........

......PEOPLE WHO COMPLAIN.......

...AND TRAFFIC-WARDENS.

The SAGITTARIAN in love........

.....IS VERY PERSISTENT........

........LIKES VARIETY..................

......IS EXPERIMENTAL.............

....ENJOYS GIVING GIFTS...........

.......IS VERY CHOOSY..............

.......SELF - CENTRED..................

.....DOESN'T LIKE ROUTINE.......

....CAN BECOME JEALOUS..........

..........IS SHY.........................

...AND VERY PASSIONATE.

SAGITTARIAN AND PARTNER

HEART RATINGS

♥♥♥♥♥ WOWEE!!

♥♥♥♥ GREAT, BUT NOT 'IT'

♥♥♥ O.K.—COULD BE FUN

♥♥ FORGET IT

♥ RUN THE OTHER WAY—FAST!

♥♥♥♥♥

ARIES LEO

♥♥♥♥

CAPRICORN LIBRA SCORPIO
AQUARIUS

♥♥♥

PISCES SAGITTARIUS

♥♥

GEMINI VIRGO

♥

TAURUS CANCER

SAGITTARIUS PEOPLE

WOODY ALLEN : FRANK SINATRA
BEETHOVEN : TOULOUSE-LAUTREC
HARPO MARX : TOMMY STEELE
JANE FONDA : WALT DISNEY
NOËL COWARD : MARK TWAIN

SIR WINSTON CHURCHILL
BRENDA LEE : EDNA O'BRIEN
JOHN PIPER : RONNIE CORBETT
IRA GERSHWIN : CHARLES SHULZ
SAMMY DAVIS JNR : KIRK DOUGLAS
SIR RALPH RICHARDSON
BORIS KARLOFF : DONALD DUCK
SIR LAURENS VAN DER POST
JOHN OSBORNE : MARIA CALLAS
LIV ULLMAN : ARTHUR C. CLARKE
BENJAMIN DISRAELI : BILLY THE KID